I0152991

# Building Cities of Gold

## Barry Fitzgerald

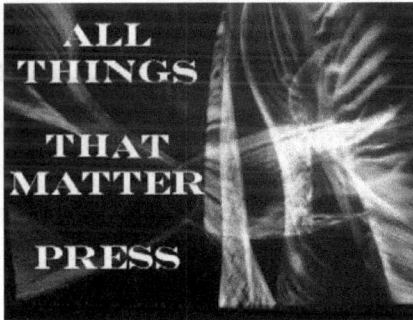

ALL
THINGS
THAT
MATTER
PRESS

Building Cities of Gold
Copyright © 2010 by Barry Fitzgerald

All rights reserved. No part of this book may be reproduced or transmitted in any form or by any means without written permission of the author and publisher.

All fictional characters and places are the product of the author's imagination. Any resemblance to actual places or persons, living or dead, is purely coincidental.

ISBN: 978-0-9846154-7-6

Library of Congress Control Number: 2010911661

Cover design by: All Things That Matter Press

Published in 2010 by All Things That Matter Press

To my children, Michael and Cara.
I guess you wouldn't be very interested in this book now, considering your ages. For you Michael, it wouldn't have enough stories about the antics and capers of your beloved trains and cars. For you Cara, it wouldn't have enough pictures of cute little puppy dogs. However like all kids today, you guys are teaching me and your mom daily. You represent the future human. The people who will live by truth, integrity and love. It is amazing to watch how you guys, and your little peers everywhere, refuse to bow to the fear and control of the existing world. Kids everywhere are teaching us adults, about love and freedom. We are humbled by your presence. You are inspiring us to change your future world, for the better.
We will try to make it happen.
To Orla. Thank you from the bottom of my heart for all your encouragement, love, support and belief in me. Since the day we met, you have always graciously allowed me the time and space to follow my dreams, whatever they may be. That is a rare quality, and proof to me of your wisdom, compassion and maturity. I love you very much and look forward greatly to our shared evolving destiny.

**City of Gold** *(English Dictionary description from the year 2100)* – Colloquial term used to describe a healthy, vibrant and sustainable community of people. Personal empowerment and integrity are considered cornerstones of these communities. Shared resources, bartering, community integration of all demographics, internal conflict resolution, community planning, alternative education and childcare programs are some common facets of daily life. Shifting of power away from conventional institutions like governments and religion into the hands of the individual and local communities is key to their success. As personal integrity levels rise, abuse of power diminishes.

Resulting from repeated economic meltdowns, organic proliferation of these communities happened in the early decades of the 21st Century. By mid century, major metropolises like London and New York had hundreds of active sustainable communities within their borders, comprising 100-200 hundred people each. There were fewer quantities of communities in the smaller cities, towns, suburbs and in the countryside due to smaller populations relative to the bigger cities. However, wherever a sustainable community existed, they all tended to operate on the same basic principles.

As the century drew to a close, these communities became the dominant organising structure in society. They had become mainstream.

# Table of Contents

# INTRODUCTION

It is the year 2010 and the world seems to be collapsing around us. More questions are being posed, than answers given. Institutions are failing; specifically financial, religious and governmental organisations worldwide.

Should we despair? Is life over as we know it? Will we revert to some semblance of stability in the near future? Will we ever experience peace and good times as common threads in our lifetimes? Does anyone care enough to lead us out of this mess? Is any one individual capable of forging through the morass and debris to bring us collectively to clear open waters?

It is easy to be consumed by despair. I believe though that our futures *can* and *will* be entirely positive, if we so choose. Please join me on my voyage through many of the social, political and environmental topics that affect our daily lives. You will see the common thread in my book is that I believe the only solution for this planet, and for us as a species is for each individual to "own" their own lives; to stand up for themselves, to partake, to have a goal and a plan, to have a guaranteed and defined role in society, to have passion, and most of all, to be optimistic. If we do the work individually as above, then the desired society changes are inevitable.

Many are trying to force us into a supposed "green" lifestyle as a one stop cure for the entire planet's problems. I believe that while there are definite positive attributes to following the way of green living, there are also downsides. The most obvious downside is that we may well create a green consumerist bubble within the next ten years.

Going "green" should be something so much more wholesome than that; it should involve a total reunion with the earth that nurtures us, with the community that sustains us and ultimately with the most important person in our world – a reunion with ourselves. Adopting green technologies and a green lifestyle will certainly be part of the journey of the future, but it is not the only destination needed for us to really mature safely, securely and happily into that future.

\*\*\*

Our perception of history as humans is confined to the immediate and that which affects us individually. It is very hard for us to understand or be empathic towards the lives of any of our ancestors prior to the generation of our grandparents. It's an alien planet for us. We believe everything has always been as it is for us. We buy into our system and way of operating in the world and never understand that it was different or that it could change or evolve again.

Our current society has been structured on one main premise for the last one hundred years or so. All the rest of human history prior to that differs from the 20th century. The common thread in the past century is the almost rigid belief we hold that our economies will grow on average at around 4%[1]. This has only been possible with one main ingredient feeding the equation; that being rapid population growth. After all, with more people in the world, we end up with more markets to sell to. We can also source more labour easily to maximise profits. People then end up being the cannon fodder to feed the insatiable beast that is the worldwide economy. This model ends up as a strict tiered hierarchy with the very rich at the top, down to the very poor at the bottom. As an example, a common statistic is that 1% of the world's population own a combined 20% of the wealth in the world[2].

There are many inherent flaws in this system. The most obvious one concerns population growth. If, as predicted[3] in and around the year 2050, our worldwide population peaks at around 10 billion people, what then happens to economic theory?

If the population peaks and then starts to decline, then surely by the late decades of this century we will be experiencing major problems whereby we have more and more diminishing markets to source our cheap labour from, and consequently, less markets to sell our products to. Our economies could then start to shrink and we will need to learn some harsh lessons the hard way.

It would appear that no government or organisation tasked with running economies is looking that far ahead. All they are concerned with is the current year and the next few years after that. Long term planning is not something that concerns these people. I contend that if this inevitable population peak occurs, then this is the greatest threat to our economic and social stability, considering the reliance we put on population growth.

There is immense irony in those currently in power telling us on the one hand that rapidly increasing population levels are threatening the environment and making access to natural resources more difficult, then on the other hand, they are running economies in such a way that the only successful evolution of those economies is to have larger and larger populations.

Basically, we need to wean ourselves off this false golden rule; the falsity that it is inevitable that our economies will constantly expand. We need to find a more solid basis to run our world. The great economic crash in late 2008 should provide a salutary lesson to us. However thus far, very few of those who have the power to change our modus operandi are seizing the chance to do so. We are valiantly trying to recover, re-ignite, re-inflate and return to the good days of the past decades. Every single stimulus package is trying to return us to the same type of economy that got us into this mess in the first place!

Could it be that a return to those days is the last thing we should be doing? I *certainly* believe so. This type of economy continuously pits us all against each other. We compete for jobs, we fear for our jobs when we have them, we don't trust in the future and we feel no security. We have no true defined role in society; we have no guaranteed place. We can have a job but it can be taken from us by any number of outside influences. That is not how things should be. It keeps most people trapped in a state of constant fear – save for the false security felt by people during the worldwide boom of 2004-2008 – and perpetuates the existing system.

What is the alternative? It cannot just be confined to an overhaul of how our economies run, but rather there needs to be an overhaul of how we value humans and our individual roles. It involves retrofitting to a sustainable lifestyle. A lifestyle that *guarantees* all of us a place, a function and a role in our society, from cradle to grave. This is not a desire for a return to the days of socialist theory that was supposed to meet the needs of all people equally, but failed dismally. That failure resulted from the holding of power in the hands of the few, to the detriment of the many. The only long term political, economic and social model that will work for us as a planet is a system that puts the power of the world in the hands of *all* the individuals.

To do something so bold, we as individuals, need to step up to the mark. Can we handle power? Unfortunately, for most people the answer is a resounding no. The thought of having the freedom to choose exactly how to live their lives, how to order society, how to plan for societies future, scares people. That is why we are so willing to hand our power over to institutions that fail us miserably. And yet, we still give them our power.

***

Climate change is being portrayed as being the single greatest danger facing mankind. While it is not understood fully, it is being linked directly to many causes. Some of those causes seem to be man made, and are most likely related to increasing population and consumption levels. Yet, we need more and more people to generate taxes, to purchase goods, to work and to sell to, so we can feed the monster that is our current economic model. Therefore, we just won't be able to make any true dents in arresting man made climate change with increasing population levels in the next fifty years in our current society models. Our mindset will need to change.

To solve these problems, the people of the world will need to reclaim their individual power. By doing so, they will put themselves in a position where they can refuse to make the choices that will contribute to more problems in the world, like the aforementioned climate change.

The biggest show in town for the next few decades needs to be our ascension into our individual power. If we can do this with integrity, humility and honesty, we will fix many of the problems of the world as a guaranteed consequence of taking full conscious responsibility for our own lives. Arresting climate change, or at least the parts of it caused by mankind, will be something that gets tackled as a natural consequence of this. If we don't strive for personal empowerment, then we are constantly waiting to be told or directed what to do in life. Therefore, something like addressing climate change becomes a task that is too incomprehensible for us to tackle, and hence, we ignore it and switch off. In this instance, we have no power.

If we do become powerful, then we become positive agents of change in our own lives and we will stop being so passive. We will stop trusting that all the institutions we currently give our power to have our best interests at heart. We will demand more from them, and if they fail us, then we will change them.

Many people worldwide were swept up in the hysteria surrounding the election of President Obama in the US in late 2008. His mantra was adopted into everyday life; that of "Yes We Can". In truth, though his message was much deeper than that. This proved to be a sound bite that was easily rolled out to describe his campaign, but if his speeches were analysed, he constantly referred to the need for the individual to step up to the mark and to stop expecting society to do everything for them[4]. His election was seen as a crumbling of the old ways because of his colour. But in time, I believe his election will be seen as something bigger than this. Here is a main political figure who is challenging us all, i.e. the individuals of the world, to create better lives for ourselves and for our local and wider community.

*** 

In part one of this book I describe the different ways we could envisage and actually have a true, sustainable lifestyle and society. This incorporates areas like the economy, education, work, family life and community life. Obviously, it can seem daunting to look at how bad things are today and look to the future and imagine a society that could be so much better. The journey between both locations can seem totally overwhelming, and so we despair and give up.

That is the very reason that prompted me to write about how people living today, in 2010, can start to take the small but rewarding steps towards living sustainable lives, even if they are living in poorly planned and unsustainable housing developments.

Therefore, by highlighting various fictional character representations we can try to implement fixes or solutions that can and will make their lives easier. Once the process starts, it won't finish until our collective task is completed. Remember the old saying about the journey of a thousand miles just needing one step to start.

We will look therefore, in Part Two, at the struggles of people like the young married couple juggling parenthood and working lives; the single elderly man isolated from society; the young teenager lost in a sea of confusing emotions unable to find clarity, and also how the loss of employment can have such a devastating effect on the lives of people. Each person has a story to tell, and each should have a secure place in our society.

In Part Three we take a look at how these fictional characters' lives would continue to play out if we hadn't implemented "fixes" for them in their daily lives. Things end up staying exactly the way they are for all of these people, and hence they allow the same dysfunctional cycles to perpetuate in their lives.

*\*\**

The change is here, we cannot hide anymore. It is time for us as individuals and as societies to create heaven on earth, and build our very own *Cities of Gold*.

Some of the concepts in my book may be familiar to you already. That's okay. I don't claim to own any information. In fact, I don't believe anyone does. The more I see of this world, the more I am convinced that all the ideas we get as humans are first formed in the ether surrounding us and, depending on the various sensitivities of people, are then downloaded by them as they tune into particular topics of interest to them. It explains why people in various parts of the world often work on very similar topics without ever having worked together or shared progress.

# PART ONE

# One: Grass Roots Solutions

It will take time, but we are going to see the evolution of communities and a society that incorporate some, or all of the ideas below.

Key facets of a true Sustainable Community:

- Aligning of people with similar goals and desires into community, preferably in close physical proximity, i.e. neighbours, but not necessarily so (up to 150 people [1]or so).
- Setting up of a barter type economy within the community – stemming from an honest appraisal of skill sets and available talents of all members.
- Barter economy has knock on effect of reducing power of cash and will reduce people's individual debt levels.
- Building of shared community buildings – some people can work from here instead of commuting to distant workplaces.
- Retrofitting of green technologies into our existing buildings to generate electricity, recycle water and process waste.
- Communal food production, even in our cities (roof gardens) – some community members employed solely in this task.
- Space in community building can be used to sell excess production of community members to wider community.
- Use of community building for shared social gatherings.
- Bringing pre-school child care back into the local community.
- Provide alternative to mainstream education in the community. This means setting up a structured school pattern that involves a mix of classroom based education and practical life affirming sessions with chosen community members.
- Do not rely entirely on barter system, in fact a proportion of community members would still work in wider society.
- Break free of 9-5 regime in careers in wider society. Renegotiate terms and conditions and seek payment for services rendered rather than time on the job.

- Become more efficient on the job, thereby freeing up more time. The more time that can be freed up, the more money is saved. Also, one can now dedicate more time to the community.
- Have community based decision making. Respect decisions of all, including both young and old.
- Represent ideas and decisions to wider society. These communities of 150 people or so will mushroom everywhere. In time, a critical mass of sustainable communities will be reached. At this point the ideas of the individual communities are now becoming mainstream. Therefore, politically they are a force.
- This political movement could take two people from each community and merge with two representatives from every other community. These representatives now truly hold the views of all individuals in society. No longer does party politics dominate our society.
- Generate medium term community plans (five years) and long term plans (fifty years).
- Generate country wide plans. Align with other countries. Have a world wide community plan and long term worldwide goal.
- Let every significant choice in life be made with the consideration of the impact on future generations.

As mentioned this is daunting, getting from where we are to the life that is described above. The evolution of society along the lines above or similar is *going* to happen. *There is only so much abuse people can take before eventually they will crack and demand change. Our recent history has all been about pursuing individual selfish goals; however, the desire for community and major reform is almost palpable in the air in 2010.* The more conscious of the process of change, the better off we are. Every man, woman and child in our world has become too isolated from their society and from their connection with the earth. Individual ascension into our own power needs to be the new mantra for us all. The evolution of the individual into personal power will result in a strong desire to connect and share with others.

Many people would baulk at this stage at the thought of being in an active community with their neighbours or their colleagues. They could list countless cases of individuals who have some personality fault or indeed they could just find reasons not to want to work and share with those people. However, those days have to end. Those people with the faults are actually all of us; therefore, all of us individually have to start owning up to our shortcomings and endeavour to evolve past them.

If our future community based society is to work, then some examples of the people who have to change are outlined below. These people may feel they are benign in their daily lives, but their current way of living is not helping society.

- The older people who wish to drain their families, seeking pity due to their advancing age, must stop this. They fail to see they have a strong role to play in our future where they pass knowledge and life experience to our youth, if we (society) allow them adopt such a role.
- The man who is a workaholic because he is afraid to stop and face him demons and emotions is going to have to do just that to become a healthy participant for himself and his family in future society.
- The adults who guide their children into unsuitable careers to sooth their own fears about security must stop. They need to allow their children find their own niche in life, regardless of that outcome, i.e. allow them mature into their rightful destiny.
- The purveyors of religion who coerce and force people to do things against their wishes in society will have to change their ways.
- The owners of large businesses that pollute our planet need to realise their deeds are detrimental to all of society and not wanted anymore.
- The teenagers and young adults who hide in the abuse of drugs and alcohol, that is so prevalent in our world, need to

find the courage to ask for our assistance as a society, to help them mature safely into their adulthood.

- The woman who is forcing herself into an early grave because she is constantly striving to be perfect in both the home and at the workplace needs to learn to stop and prioritise her goals (whatever they may be) in life.

We all have a story. Everyone knows where they are lacking and where they need to change to become healthy members of a community. This is the evolution of us as individuals that has to happen to enable true sustainable community with our neighbours. Perhaps, then, we would not baulk at the notion of sharing our lives with our fellow man.

We need to form community to survive. It will be our trump card. Let's now start looking at some areas of true sustainable community in more detail.

## Two: The Earth Provides

Our economic models are not totally crazy. In fact, the concepts are quite smart. Namely, that the amount of money circulating on the globe should match the value of all the goods and services in circulation. Debt arises when we bank on the value of these assets rising in the future and, therefore, this allows us to feel confident to borrow money from the future to use today. Inevitably, we end up paying a lot more in return than we borrowed. This interest allows the future supply of money to grow, too. Unfortunately, a system like this is highly susceptible to confidence. If we feel confident, we can borrow and trust our ability to pay in the future. If we feel scared and confidence is low, we do exactly the opposite and future growth will also start to slow.

What people fail to see in this rollercoaster of a ride is that everything comes from the earth. We do not trade with any other planet, as far as I am aware!

So if everything we use, source, build, sell or purchase is from the earth, then how come economies are so volatile? After all, the earth itself does not follow economic trends. It yields its bounties like water, wood, food, minerals, oil and gas freely. We then use these commodities to live and grow.

There is not a single item in the world that is not derived from one of the base raw materials the earth provides so willingly for us. People will argue that not everything is from the earth, that this is a ridiculous concept. Surely, the guys who write advanced software programs or the surgeon who uses the most advanced leading edge surgical equipment are using mans ingenuity.

This may seem true and indeed, mans' ingenuity has been outstanding throughout history. However, the software engineer above is typing on a laptop (that is plastic, derived from petrochemicals or oil). The life in the laptop is provided from electricity that comes from power lines (made of copper, an earth derived metal), supported by poles (timber) and coming from a power plant (built from concrete blocks, derivative of stone from the earth). This is most likely using a fossil fuel (gas) to burn, to generate the electricity.

You see, it all breaks down to everything we use or do, being *of* the earth. Similarly, for the surgeon or anyone else going about their daily tasks. The earth does not ask us for payment for any of this. It never has, nor ever will.

We will see in a subsequent chapter that many people have died in the name of defending their God or religion. The feats their Gods could perform were seen as miraculous. However, to me the real miracle is that the earth where we all play out our lives is nurturing us continuously. That this hardened globe of rock and seas spinning and travelling at crazy speeds through the skies has got exactly the right combination of life supporting mechanisms is a miracle beyond belief.

But we take it so much for granted. The earth has been here for billions of years, it will be here for billions more. It has sustained life forms we don't know anything about. It will support life forms in the future that are totally alien to us.

The bounties of the world sustain us fully. Water, fruits, vegetables, wood, stone and minerals to name a few are the building blocks of everything. If it is not provided in a format that we can use we then apply our ingenuity to transform it into something we can utilise. That is wonderful to know; we on planet earth have everything we need!

But do we have enough for everyone?

# Three:  Will the Earth Provide in the Future?

That is the one major leap of faith left. I don't know the answer to that question. Nobody does. One has to believe, though, that in the world as it is today, the answer is a definite no to this question. How could there be enough with the levels of consumption we pursue. As mentioned already, there are 6 billion of us, rising up to 10 billion within fifty years[1]. If we changed our fundamental relationship with the bounties of the earth, then maybe there could be enough resources for us all.

The only one capable of answering that question is the earth itself. Since it has such an advanced self regulatory system, one could believe that it has all of the resources required for all of these people as it has birthed them into being. It is she[2] who is testing us, I believe, not the other way around. She can handle us; she wants us to prove we can handle each other. At the moment, we are like unruly kids running amok. Yet, like any mother, she is waiting patiently for us to grow up and mature to the point where we do not carry on like this.

So if the earth provides us with all the raw materials we need, and if we can make the leap of faith to believe she will provide all we need in the future, then why do we have unemployment, scarcity and lack among so many and so much in the hands of so few? Who decided at what point that access to all of these resources would have to be controlled through so few hands? Someone, somewhere did and we have all fed into that belief system ever since!

We have been led to believe that our economy is only sustainable if we keep working, keep purchasing, keep borrowing and keep consuming. This is not natural law. The earth will yield her bounty, but at the moment we cannot handle that bounty. We need a whole new reprogramming to learn how to distribute the yield fairly.

A good analogy for the way we live our lives is to think of the seas. Our daily lives, and especially our economies, inhabit the choppy waters at the surface that are subjected to highs and lows from waves and winds. We are always unsure, are we on the crest or facing into a trough?

However, beneath us we have this great mass or body of water that is very calm and sure of itself. It can support anything it wants and is not subject to the whims of the surface. That is a very similar snapshot for our relationship with the earth that sustains us. We are on the surface, totally unsure of ourselves and we are running around like headless chickens. We lack the confidence or knowledge to know that this great mass beneath us has the answers to all our worries and will provide for us if we allow it to.

# Four: Can We Decouple from Our Current Path?

We know that all the goods and services in the world are derived from the raw materials and bounty of the earth. In our current society and economic model, we hope to become educated enough and get lucky enough to get a job somewhere high up on the food chain. Once there, we can use less brawn and more brain to fashion, design, sell and trade goods and services to others for profit.

We are told this is the only path to success: to become more and more ruthless and competitive so we can claw and inch higher and higher up the ladder. Obviously, as you do so, you are using others as your foundations, those with less education, less luck, less competitive instincts or those of a meeker constitution.

*So can we decouple from this madness?*

In my introduction, I mentioned the next few decades were going to see the greatest industry of the 21st century; that of a move to a sustainable society. I believe we can decouple from the madness, but unfortunately, it will take several generations to do so fully. The young adults of 2090 will still be working diligently on this project.

Primarily, we have to move ownership of resources back to *all* the people (not to some flawed socialist model as outlined in the introduction). One way this is already starting to happen is from the back end. Bill Gates and Warren Buffet, between them, are planning to pump close to 100 billion dollars of profit from the current economic system back into education, health and environmental causes worldwide, but especially so in the third world. This is very laudable and these are obviously very advanced souls to be able to relinquish their power in this manner. However, would there be a need for them to do this if the resources that made their wealth (and that of others) in the first instance had gone to communal hands. That is the crux. Philanthropy is fantastic, but does philanthropy work in a flawed system?

Will the poorest of the poor who benefit in dollar terms from these donations actually secure a future for themselves where they can be independent, access everything they need and have security of resources for the future? Unfortunately, I don't believe they will. It might build much valued shelter, give much needed healthcare, or much appreciated education, but it does not equip those people to safely say they can survive the rest of their days without needing somebody else to employ them (who can subsequently fire them) or provide for them. In essence, it is endeavouring to help raise them up to living their lives at the economic levels of the western world. This is certainly a laudable goal, but many people in the western world feel totally afraid, lost and insecure. Their conditions are far from stable and even though they live in a supposed advanced society, they are often weeks or months away from destitution[1].

And so we reach the crux of what we need to do. What is required is that each of us can access *any* resource we may need throughout our lifetimes and trust that it will always be available. We also need to trust that we have the power within ourselves to provide for ourselves and our families, from cradle to grave. Nobody should have the power to take away our economic security at a whim, or due to some trend on a balance sheet.

If we can manage to gain this self security, where we are confident we will always be able to provide for ourselves and our families for the rest of our lives, then we can live much freer and happier lives. In essence, we need to know that we will always be able to access our fair share of the earth's bounty and, also, that there will always be a need for our skills and services in the world. If we can get to this point, we will have successfully decoupled from our current path.

*** 

## Summary

### Current Society Beliefs:
- Increasing population levels mean we will run out of resources.
- Disconnection with bounty of Earth. People don't see that all resources ultimately come from the Earth.

- Individuals have no right or control over access to resources of the earth.
- Individuals need to compete against each other continuously for bounty of the earth, be it in the form of jobs, money, or goods and services.

**Sustainable Community Beliefs:**

- Trust that Earth can sustain all of mankind, if we learn to distribute yield fairly.
- Respect and keen insight in to lifecycle and source of all our produce.
- Resources of earth should be available for all of the people throughout their lives.
- Everyone has a place in society that is guaranteed from cradle to grave. Security of access to resources (in whatever form) is considered a basic human right.

# Five: What is a Sustainable Economy?

A sustainable economy is not one that is tied to a requirement like the need for continued population increase. Rather, it is one that can keep the flow of money and resources moving indefinitely without forcing people unnecessarily out of work during down periods or suffering from over exuberant boom periods. The people trust in its ability to meet their needs; like going to a well and pulling up just the amount of water needed at that moment. *Of course this ties in with reaching a certain level of personal empowerment and maturity; one only accesses that which is needed and not ever exploitatively.*

Imagine if we have reached a plateau in many inputs to an economy, i.e. we are all as well educated as we can be, we are all as technically proficient as we can be, and we are all earning very good salaries. There doesn't seem to be any room for growth. Currently, we are told that this signifies a death sentence for the economy. The long and steady decline to oblivion. Sustainability though, is exactly what needs to take over here, as it is the ability to maintain ourselves without the need for constantly changing inputs. Remember when the population starts to shrink, then, with our current model we *are* doomed for failure. However, if we have a sustainable economic system, then we can maintain ourselves.

An example from my own life would be my work in multinational corporations. We would get something working nicely on a production line and I would be quite content to then leave this "fix" in place indefinitely, even if it was not ideal. My thoughts were always that it was fine, so why tinker with it again? However, there was always pressure from above to improve, to change, to evolve, get leaner, more efficient and quicker. The belief system was that if we didn't stop innovating, we would die. The reason to innovate was to pump out more and more product to further increase profits.

Around this time, I would slink off for a coffee to the canteen (to dream) and I remember that a constant thought in my head throughout those years was that at some point, we would run out of people to sell to. How can you keep growing and growing and growing unless we suddenly tapped the emerging markets on Mars, Pluto and Venus!

This work ethic was not sustainable.

And sure enough, it never is. Manufacturing tends to last a maximum of twenty years in a particular location before the factory shuts down, or else it moves to newer and cheaper labour force markets. It is almost a rule of thumb.

If output and profit were not the only guiding factors, then these factories could perhaps stay in place for the working life of people. So what if profit growth flat lined or moved up and down year to year. If they are supplying a valuable commodity to the market, then they should morally be obliged to stay in business to keep those people in employment and to serve their markets. A rush to close off businesses that do not meet pre-defined profits is simply the stuff of lunacy. And yet, we accept this daily.

As an aside, look at the current economic meltdown in the world. Downsizing is the new buzz word and even profitable businesses are laying off staff and shutting down sections of their operations. A lot of opportunism is happening where companies figure it is a perfect time to save themselves money by laying off staff or closing down business units. They are smart enough to know that with so much bad news in the world, they will escape a public backlash for doing something like this. And they are correct. How can they get a lashing from their workers or from the general public when businesses everywhere are shutting down? I am not saying all companies are doing this, and there are certainly many people valiantly doing everything to retain their loyal staff, but there are plenty who see it is a major opportunity for exploitation.

*** 

That brings us to the main ingredient that needs to change to move us as a society to a sustainable economy. We need to get away from our addiction to money. We spoke a little earlier about how this piece of paper is used as a representation to trade goods. A higher value written on one piece of paper compared with another means it can buy more goods.

I wonder what an alien visiting us might think of this. Two identical looking pieces of paper with different abilities to purchase. Money in the form of cash has become King, but it has no intrinsic value of its own. The paper itself is pretty much valueless. It is the representation on it that brings value to it. Hence, perceptions can change the relative buying power of these pieces of paper, (e.g. currency fluctuations on stock markets). Powerful individuals or corporations can manipulate these values at a whim.

The answer, I believe, is to move back to a much stricter valuation system for goods and services. The idea of a fixed quantity of the earth's natural resources, having a fixed monetary value[1] is very credible. This could be any of the natural bounties like timber, water, oil or gas or indeed many others. A basket of these goods could become the standard valuation mechanism. These valuations would be fixed and pegged to a single currency for a period of say, ten years, after which they would be reviewed again. Therefore, we would not be susceptible to the wild vagaries of inflation and deflation.

*** 

Another valuable weapon in the move to sustainable economics is to reintroduce the notion of barter. Each of us has unique skill sets. If we can work for each other with no cash transactions, then it negates the need to have to borrow money to perform bigger tasks in life. Imagine if, like the Quakers or Amish, we all assisted each other to build our homes how debt free we could be. No longer would we have outrageous mortgages repayments. We would only have to pay for the goods themselves. Straight away we are taking the power away from money and putting it into our own hands. In such a system, people do not have to work as hard or as long in their lifetimes in their career of choice as they are not paying back huge excessive mortgages with added interest. Obviously, we have to give back in return, i.e. our time and labour to assist others. This doesn't have to "cost" us anything financially, as we can do it during our fallow times where very often we may just be wasting time anyway.

We will see in a later chapter how governments will also need to evolve with the advent of sustainable communities. If we have a barter system as part of our economy, it suddenly means there are far less tax revenues payable to the coffers of government. However, if people are working for each other in communities, it will ultimately imply that government doesn't need to play such a big role in peoples' lives and, hence, will not need the current high levels of tax revenue it takes to run our countries. Therefore, in this evolutionary process, big government will shrink over time alongside the rise in prominence of local communities.

It is a matter, therefore, of taking our power back from money – cash. I am not advocating the abolishment of cash or the ability to earn cash for services rendered. What I am saying is that it holds far too much power in our world. Cash is not King. We let it be, but it is a poor pretender to the throne.

Money, in its current form, should only influence a percentage of our economy. If we moved more and more to a barter type economy, then its power automatically diminishes. We could then safely envisage a future where bartering could become half of all economic transactions, and the conventional cash/credit market would run the other half of the economy. This would be a more sustainable long term model.

\*\*\*

Another thing a true sustainable economy needs to do is to discourage the hoarding of cash and assets that is taking place in our current economic model. Money should be something that circulates freely in exchange for goods and services. As it comes in, so it goes out. Like a lake receiving water from a waterfall, but then yielding it down a valley via a river. There is a flow, but yet there is a guaranteed supply of water in the lake for all to partake.

We need to adopt a similar belief in money. "I will not hoard this paper, I will let it go freely because there will always be more". If we all truly believed that statement in our hearts, there would be no more poverty. Why? Because we would believe we all can access the resource that is money whenever we so wished. It is like the deep pool above, we would just dip in and take what we need. *Note: It is not just confined to cash as the same is true of accessing goods and services and also for the offering of our own goods and services. The bottom line is we have a trust that we will be catered for.*

Imagine if the pool got clogged on the way to the river. Pretty quickly it would back up and get murky, stale and overflow to cause damage. This is exactly what happens with money. As the few who have lots of it hoard it, then it cannot serve those downstream and the hoarding of it doesn't bring them any great joy, either. It often clouds or muddies their lives.

Therefore, perhaps we should make money or cash devalue if we hold onto it for too long. If we keep money tied up out of our economy, it can't assist others and so we should be penalised for this. Our money should possibly now be able to buy fewer goods than it did before. This is the opposite of what happens now whereby one gains interest on stored capital. But how does that stored capital serve society? The simple answer is it doesn't beyond being a resource that banks use to then allow them loan out more and more money to people, thereby trapping yet more people into large interest repayments.

*** 

One of the main reason why our free market economy has been accepted by the masses for so long is that it gives people the belief that if they work hard enough, get lucky enough, or step on enough toes, then invariably, they will one day become rich beyond their wildest dreams and be able to live a life of luxury. In reality, only a very, very small percentage of people make this a reality. But yet the possibility of it, or indeed the promise of it, is enough to make the majority of people accept it as the best way to run a society's economy.

In the model of a sustainable economy, the promise is not that you, the individual might achieve all you wish, but more so that all of the people in society can attain much more secure and guaranteed resources for themselves and their families. Instead of the few getting everything, the many gain security. Again, this is not a harking to a socialist model that still exploits everyone, but for a sounder, more even distribution of the assets of the world.

***

## Summary

### Current Society Economy:
- Growth is all that is tolerated, to the detriment of everything. Society will crash if contraction sets in for prolonged periods with the way this society is structured.
- Cash (money) is King. It trumps everything else. Hence we have mad scrambles to amass this resource. It is often hoarded by people and cannot serve society if this is the case. Its value fluctuates wildly and is influenced by confidence levels on a second – second basis.
- Monetary transactions (cash or credit) account for nearly 100% of world's economy
- Leads to a lot of people owing large amounts of money that has been borrowed from system to pay for bigger goods and services. This keeps these people trapped into longer and longer working lives to repay money.

### Sustainable Community Economy:
- At times economies will grow; sometimes they may contract but either way it doesn't matter. Over the long term society can sustain itself regardless of economic performance.
- Power of cash diminishes by several means.
  1. Bartering; where goods and services are exchanged outside of cash economy
  2. Hoarding of cash leads to it's devaluation
  3. Currencies are pegged to a fixed quantity of the earth's bounty and not to confidence levels.
- Bartering in the local economy accounts for approximately 50% of economic activity.
- Traditional monetary economy accounts for the other 50%
- Significant amount of transactions could be obtained from barter system, thus freeing people up so they do not have

to borrow money from wider economy. This means they need to earn less money in a lifetime to repay these monies and hence they could possibly have shorter working lives.

# Six:  What is a Sustainable Career?

This is the concept that each and every one of us on this planet has a given skill set or talent level. *Obviously there are a small percentage of people incapacitated by illness who need to be looked after by the majority.* These skills can be used for our own ends or to help meet the needs of others and can be accessed whenever, wherever or for as long as we choose to do so. By performing our chosen career, we gain a standing in our community, either through the exchange of cash or the building up of credits in a barter system that we can subsequently draw from ourselves in the future.

We may have evolved greatly in the last few centuries. We see ourselves as having access to various things like fantastic diagnostic and corrective medicines, superior education levels and every technological gadget imaginable. However, in many ways we are far more trapped than any of our distant ancestors.

If we go back to ancient tribal and nomadic societies, it has been ascertained anthropologically that these people only worked on average about four hours a day[1]. This work was basically to forage for and find food. This tended to be the preserve of the men while the women prepared the fire to cook the food and tended to the children. For the rest of the time, these people enjoyed family life, performed rituals (both fun based and spiritual) and basically relaxed. Now it seems absurd, therefore, that money would have had any place in that society. Quite the opposite, theirs was a contract with the earth. They would enjoy their lives, honour the earth, and in return, the earth would always provide for them with the minimum of effort required on their part (four hours a day).

They trusted the earth would always provide. The transaction on the other side was the requirement to find the produce of the earth. Nobody was wasted in this process. If you were male, you went in search of the bounty. If you were female, you helped prepare the subsequent find. Young and old all had their place. There was no such thing as retiring. Four hours a day from cradle to grave.

One always had a role, a function and a place. Okay, one did not get to go away on two weeks break twice a year or, retire at sixty five to play golf. But, if you asked people if they would prefer to work four hours a day for the rest of their lives, or work the current 9-5 model until they were sixty five or older, which do you think they would pick? *(Remember the 9-5 is never just that. Add up to two hours each side of that eight hour day for commuting to get average working times in the Western world)*

If *all* one's needs could be met with four hours of work a day and one was guaranteed not to be thrown on the scrapheap at sixty five, then I think most people would grab this deal. Now I am not advocating that we all return to the era in history described above. We live in the 21$^{st}$ century and we need, deserve and want to keep our current standard of living. However, people are chasing their tails to maintain it all.

Therefore we need to break the model that exists. Where did, Monday-Friday 9-5 come from? It basically evolved to that point through the centuries. When the first slaves started to be kept, they were effectively considered working animals. You let these "sub humans" sleep to recuperate, but otherwise, they worked until they died. This evolved further into the industrial revolution where the only difference with the slaves was that people were at least getting paid for their labour. Aside from that, the conditions were not much better than for the poor slaves.

In time, unions came to prominence, and the labour movement improved workers rights to the point where it was considered nirvana to get two days a week off work and to only have to work eight hours a day. This became accepted as *good* working conditions and was the panacea to cure all ills. Everyone should have been delighted with these enlightened conditions. However, what we all failed to realise is that it was the evolution from slavery and still contained many of the same controls.

We are "on the clock". If we need to leave work, we have to "clock off". It is assumed everyone's own natural body clock works to this rhythm and that it suits each individual's needs. However, nothing could be further from the truth.

From my own experience, working as a nine to fiver in the past, I hated the strict routine. I always felt like we were in school or something similar, and far from being treated like adults. It often felt like we were being treated like truant children. I could sit at my desk and get the equivalent workload completed on Monday and Tuesday that another person, who was comfortable with the enforced work schedule, may take a week to complete. The end result was we would both get the same quantity of work done in a week, but I looked bad because I was "idle" for several days.

My work method has always been to do short intense bursts, with relaxation in between. Therefore, a steady work flow over five days that is suddenly turned on at 9am and finished at 5pm was anathema to me.

So many colleagues also appeared to have problems fitting in with the "schedule". People often wasted hours every day just to fill up their required scheduled day. Realistically, they probably only worked a few hours a day. Between wasteful meetings, long coffee breaks and socialising, many hours were wasted. Again, we need to rethink this model.

*** 

The idea of getting a salary for a position needs to change. We need to re-numerate people for workload, rather than for a position. If we re-numerate them on workload, it means we cut out all the excess time currently wasted in offices[2] worldwide. If one is paid 50,000 units of currency annually to work in an office as an engineer, then it is guaranteed that up to 50% of that individual's time is wasted during the work week. In theory, the company is paying for that person to drink coffee, daydream, surf the internet, stop for chats during the day, as well as doing their actual job function. In most cases these people do not want to be in the office for all the fallow periods, either. They would just like to get their job done and head home. So, if we paid people for workload and not time, it would free up a lot of extra time for the worker (this has the added benefit of allowing them the time to be active in the barter economy in their local community), and it would also make them more efficient for the employer.

With the advent of the internet, a lot of work can be done by telecommuting. Therefore, as well as paying people for workload, we can also let them choose when and where they work from. That means one person could be an early bird and fulfil their projects in the early part of the day, while another could be a night owl and fulfil their requirements at this time. If they can telecommute, it means they could be performing their job from home, on their time, at a time of their choosing.

Suddenly, we have greatly empowered people. We have broken the chains of the clock and the 9-5 cycle of working. Obviously, it can't work for everyone, but there are millions of people worldwide in positions that could be done free from the regimented clock and also could be done offsite at a time of the worker's choosing.

***

Now that just looks at the process. What is much more critical is to discuss what we all should be doing. What is our ideal career? What do we want to do for the rest of our days?

This is a big question and will be looked at later on in more detail in the chapter on education, but suffice it to say for now, very few people in the world are actually working at their ideal career. Too many followed careers that they felt would guarantee a good salary or followed careers that their peers and family felt they should pursue.

So combine a forced schedule of working the same hours day after day, week after week, month after month, and year after year, with being in the wrong career in the first place, and it is quite easy to see that many people must be very unhappy. They feel trapped, as if they have nowhere to go. It's almost like they say, "this is what I have settled for; it's best just to make the most of it".

However they could at least lobby for change regarding the structures of their work, even if they could never summon the courage to jump ship to their ideal career. Why not try to renegotiate a system where you evaluate every task you perform in your job. Try and figure out how many of these tasks could be done outside of the regimented work environment. Try to work a situation where these tasks are done on your time. Make that part of your career highly efficient, i.e. the bit you are performing on your time. The more efficient you are here, the more free time you have suddenly created in your life.

Another thing people should consider is trying to become an independent contractor in their career. To a lot of people, a guaranteed salary makes them feel very safe where a certain portion goes on taxes, a certain portion on a pension, and perhaps health insurance and the rest is net salary. However, in this they are giving an awful lot of control to other people.

One is assuming the pension is a good policy. Most people would not even know where this money is going. Ask the millions of people worldwide whose pensions were wiped out during 2008-2009 if they now consider it a good policy. Even in good economic times, very often a huge proportion of the monies paid into these schemes go on fees for the handlers. As it is not their money, they are not intimately concerned about its performance.

People are also paying a set tax level that may not be availing of all their deductions. Again, people are handing over their power to the payroll staff in their company. If they renegotiate with their employers to become independent contractors and work part of the time from home, or offsite, then as well as getting more free time, they can also get much more control over their finances.

One can still choose a pension investment scheme, but if self directed, a lot more care and attention will be put into choosing the investments. Similarly, tax returns in the control of the individual will empower them more and let them see more fully the flow of money into and out of their lives.

***

## Summary

**Current Society Career Path:**
- Very often people choose the career that pays the most, regardless of suitability. Then they try to work longer, harder and better than anyone else to get by.
- People step on others to climb the prosperity ladder.
- Constantly fear that it may all be pulled away at a moments notice by any number of outside influences.

- One working week model suits all people.
- People controlled by clock. Paid and re-numerated for quantity of time given from one's life to a job.
- Gross wastage of time to "fill up" work week, leading to disillusionment.
- People work obscene hours from 18-65 years of age. Then they are thrown on scrap heap at 65. No defined role in society thereafter.
- Defines people by salary level.
- Does not empower people as companies often handle taxes, pensions, healthcare schemes etc.

**Sustainable Community Career Path:**
- Take time early in life (see chapter on education) to discover unique skills and talents. Offer these over the course of a working life, on either barter or wider cash economy.
- No fear of it all being taken away as bartering and other measures have devalued cash, hence businesses do not pull out with the same frequency. Also barter economy ensures there is always some need for one's work even if wider economy is in a slow phase.
- Each individual has their own body clock and optimum performance times. Let people perform their workload at this time and not to a pre-defined work week for all.
- Decouple from the working clock. Re-numerate people (through either Barter or cash economy) for services rendered and not time on the job. This frees up more time for people as they are no longer being paid for time in a role or position.
- Encourages shorter working weeks of perhaps 30 hours spread over 7 days. No enforced retirement, people can choose to work in old age. Either way they will have a role at this stage of life. (barter economy)
- Empowers people to work in barter economy or in wider cash economy as sole traders. People handle their own taxes and pensions etc. to allow more ownership of their financial affairs.

# Seven:  What is Sustainable Education?

If someone left school at fifteen they would generally have the belief that they are only capable of earning a set figure per annum, e.g. let us say 20,000 units of currency. Someone who stayed in school until eighteen may figure they can earn 25,000 units of this money. A college graduate will believe they should get paid more money than either of the others and may believe they should get paid a figure like 30,000.

The point is, we limit ourselves to these figures, i.e., we value ourselves based on our ability to "earn" a set amount of this paper currency. The person who left school at fifteen is perceived by our current society to have the least earning power. However, this person may have wonderfully practical skill sets that could be of huge benefit to their local and wider community. Instead, they are pigeonholed in life based on educational performance. Of course, we all know the exception to the rule (the millionaire who left school at fifteen), but for the main, this holds true.

Sustainable education means those formative years need to become the most important stage of our lives. All children are expected to fit into the 9-3 or 9-4 Monday – Friday classroom based education system. However, it is certain that this system does not suit a significant proportion of our children.

Children have different needs, different abilities, different skill sets and different interests. Our education of them has to be holistic. By this I mean encompassing so much more than classroom based theoretical studies. Also, the pressure of certain life defining examinations at various stages of development needs to be removed.

True sustainable education utilises the knowledge of the community. Going back again to older societies, things were different. For example, the Native Americans let their children learn at the feet of the wise elders, with the adult warriors or with the home keepers. Education was about learning the skills of life, not filling little heads with facts and figures.

For us, today, we have so many resources we could adopt in this way. How many vibrant elderly people are wasting away in enforced retirement when they would love to assist society in some way? Sending groups of children on practical expeditions with these people could be a wonderful passing over of vital life affirming wisdom.

Very often, careers are chosen on the basis of the amount of security involved or on the amount of earning power available. The idea of securing permanent employment in the public sector, or indeed, a hugely lucrative career in the private sector, can seem perfect. That may be so, but nobody should choose a career based on conditions like this. If one is allowing a great life choice like this to be dictated by security of tenure or earning power, then it is guaranteed it will not be the right choice for that person.

Anybody who is earning money from their passions in life never calls it work. That may be what it is, i.e. they perform the task daily for several hours, but to them it is what they were put on this earth to do. They could quite happily do it forever. That is what we need to strive for. We need to allow our children the room to explore and express themselves until they have found their calling or skill sets.

How do we do this? As mentioned already, the elders took an active role in education in ancient societies. It involved setting tasks and missions to ascertain the various skill sets and talents of their charges. These would be carefully observed encounters and over time, many different elders would build up an understanding and intuitive appreciation of what each child had to offer.

In time, as the children turned to adulthood, they were expected to vision quest. This was where they were sent out into the wild for four days or so to survive on their own without food or water. The idea being that with the absence of these necessities, it would lighten their energy and send them into altered states where they had the ability to figure out their destiny or life path. On return from the quest, the "child" was now considered a young adult for coming through the initiation.

I am not advocating a return to that type of quest. However, there is great merit in its purpose. It greatly empowers the younger generation to feel the strength that courses through them, to gain the satisfaction of overcoming fears and phobia to survive in the wild, and to then return home with a confident vision of their role and destiny.

I believe we should formalise some sort of similar supervised maturation process between the ages of 14-18 for both boys and girls. Once we have educated our youth, we then need them to explore their boundaries to figure out where they want to go and what they want to do. We have a very mini version of this in Ireland where some students (only some as not all schools have this) of about 15-16 get one year out of the school cycle, called transition year where they get to feel this freedom. This is a great concept, but I feel it needs to expand to all children and to be of a longer period; preferably a couple of years.

If our children in the future were doing various creative and community based projects over a long enough period of time, it is a guarantee that if the correct observation and counselling was coupled with this, then each one could gently find his or her path in life and slip onto that road with ease. *I realise the path for some is the current model of formal education and a formal preparation for the traditional careers like being doctors, solicitors, accountants etc. I am not advocating these people are ignored by a solely creative based education system. They, too, can fit in with this new model for a time, but if their preference is the classroom and learning they can slip back into mainstream education.*

Unfortunately for the older generations, it was not so. If you were good at school, you progressed to college and a probable professional career. If you were not so good at formal schooling, it was expected you would leave early and pursue a manual trade. No second thought was given to the fact that the absence or presence of one narrow part of learning, i.e. academic ability, should play such a huge role in a person's whole life.

Nobody probed deeper to see that perhaps the guy who was being shipped off to a building site to become a carpenter because his grades were not up to scratch was in fact not suitable for this job. He was much too sensitive for the rough and tumble of life on a site. In fact, if he had been given the space to explore his options, he would have figured out that he loved children and had a vocation to work with little kids as they discovered the world.

Similarly, the genius who was the pride of his school ended up carrying their expectations with him as he became a top barrister but his career gave him no joy. It was only years later when he purchased a large house with an overgrown garden that he realised his vocation all along had been to be a designer of garden spaces to optimise flower, plant and food production.

Both these men could have had years of joy working in community with their neighbours and friends. Both may have become successful in their ill suited chosen careers, but the smallest chance happenings set them on their paths. The fact that they became skilled in their careers shows they were multi skilled, which so many of us are. However, the application of one skill in the wrong career choice will never make up for the loss of the missed life.

It is never too late for a break with convention, either. I have seen so many people who actually do know what their ideal career is; their passion. However, aside from not having the courage to leave their current security and career, which I understand, they refuse to even entertain the idea of at least training in their passion, something I do not understand.

I suppose, though, that if one trained up in one's passion, then inevitably a time will come where a choice will have to be made; to leave the security of the current life behind and jump into that life of passion, or to stay as things are. It can be easier to suppress and ignore those desires than to allow them into our lives.

***

The idea, too, of just being able to perform one task for an entire working life needs to change. Even if we have chosen our true passionate path in life there is nothing to say that we cannot train further, retrain, or find new passions and outlets as we mature.

Life is constantly evolving. If you are fifty, then the person you were at thirty would seem strange to you. That is because you have matured and evolved. The same could be said of the functions we perform as part of society. They, too, can evolve.

We all need to get to a place whereby we trust that our passion and our skills are enough to support us throughout our lives. This chapter ties in with the concept of a sustainable economy. If our passion is our job then it should not feel like work. Also we probably never want to retire from it. However, for this to be the case, we need to know that when we go to the well, there will always be a need for our services, we will get re-numerated in some fashion for it, and we will always have a role in our society.

If we trust in the abundance of the earth first and foremost, then we can trust in the abundance of our society. We will always have a role and a function, even in our latter days. We will always be supported materially by society, be it in the form of bartering or cash transactions.

***

## Summary

**Current Society Education Models:**
- Early school leavers are destined to earn less money in their lifetimes and therefore will have less opportunity to improve their social standing.
- Prepares people primarily for state examinations.
- Education defined as happening during a set period of the year; generally September – July and during the hours 9am- 4pm Monday through Friday.
- Very often does not meet the needs of many children as it is primarily focussed on academic ability and the need for a quick uptake of a lot of information.
- Parents often push children into ill suited careers based on their own fears of future potential loss of job or income.

**Sustainable Community Education Models:**
- School is a forum to observe the personality traits of all children and is used to tease out their unique skills and latent talents, regardless of ability.
- Prepares people for life by utilising knowledge of entire community, e.g. older people could barter time to teach

children life skills.

- Education is a lifelong process for all, but for young people it becomes more spread out and is not tied to strict timelines. It becomes part of their life without them even realising it.
- Students who would be considered weak in the traditional model do not get left behind as alternative learning techniques are utilised. These could incorporate more practical work and field trip type activities with community members.
- More community members take an active role in educating children; hence more people have an opinion on their skills and talents.
- Children themselves have stronger idea of their preferred route from the time and space they were given.
- Since economies are more sustainable and since barter is so strong, fear over future earnings, and career prospects are far less influential.

# Eight:   The Roles of Men and Women

There is no doubt that throughout history either men or women have been in the ascendancy over the other sex at various times. We often wrongly assume that just because men held a lot of the power through the last number of centuries that it was always so. That is not true. Again, through anthropological studies, it has been ascertained that women were the leaders in society at other times; ancient Egypt being an example.

The feminist movement has quite rightly tried to right the wrongs perpetrated on women through recent history, starting with the struggles for suffrage a century ago. This was a very necessary step to swing the pendulum of power away from the male dominated powerbase. The only problem with swinging a pendulum is it obviously passes through the balance point and over to the other side several times before it settles at the balance or middle point.

What is the balance point? Well, it is the point at which men and women can coexist in mutual harmony. It is where neither sex threatens the other. In simple terms, it could mean men are totally comfortable allowing women to hold powerful positions in the workplace, and women are totally comfortable allowing men hold a powerful position in the home. *By powerful I mean the healthy description of that word, i.e. full of power used for positive purposes.*

If we look at the history of the past few hundred years, it can be very easy to blame all men as the villains for keeping women in powerless situations. However, in most cases, the husbands, brothers and fathers of those women were also in totally powerless situations. They worked long hours in unsafe, dreary and miserable conditions. Women worked in similar miserable positions, but in the home. It was the power of the few[1] that kept both sexes powerless. One of the only privileges the men had over the women was the power to vote, but even that came quite late for the masses.

I believe the one advantage women received from this long period was the strong bonds of sisterhood. As women toiled in the home performing horribly laborious tasks that we take for granted today, they had a strong sense of solidarity. Unfortunately, I don't believe the same was true of men. They worked in factories or in mines or in similarly tough physical conditions and never shared their joys, sorrows and woes. It left a poor legacy that lasts right through to today, where men often feel isolated and unable to handle their emotions.

My point is that both sexes are dealing with the legacy of a dysfunctional system. Both men and women were kept powerless throughout history. We are both trying to figure out our future roles in society. That is my only concern with any discussion of the role and function of sexes in society today. Unfortunately, any present day discussion on the role of the sexes seems strongly weighted towards the concerns, fears and roles of women. Like I mentioned in the pendulum analogy, I believe this is a natural step we are going through where women are reclaiming a large portion of power, especially in relation to their role in the workplace. However, we also need to understand that the role of men has become very murky, watered down, and they are very often totally unsure of where society needs them or what their role in society actually is.

We need a situation where both sexes can lay claim to an equal role in society. Today, too many males are weighed down by an inherited guilt for being men, hence the feeling of needing to atone for past sins against women, while women are weighed down by so many expectations, now that their horizons are opened.

If we look at our analogy in the chapter on sustainable careers regarding work needing to be a part of our lives, and not the totally dominant force, then we can see how this would dovetail beautifully with the needs of the individual, but even more so for the family.

Most women talk today about the absolute crazy schedules they are trying to maintain to have both a successful career and a happy and healthy home life. If we were to look at the idea of less work being required to earn our way in society, i.e. the four hour a day analogy, then this would fit in perfectly with the desires of women to keep valuable time free for the family. Most women will confess to desiring their independence and standing outside the home, but hating the time commitments involved. This would be the perfect solution.

Men have inherited all the legacy of the manual labourer toiling in the factories and mines. Because they traditionally never had a strong role in the daily running of a household, the question of the work life balance has been less of a concern for them.

However, it is time for that to change, too. Men can often hide in their work, using it as an excuse to avoid other areas of their lives they do not wish to dwell on or illuminate. In a lot of cases, they need to step more up to the mark and take more of an active role in the family. Here the concept of reduced workload outside the home works wonderfully to allow them to do this.

If both men and women were to avail of shorter more productive working lives, they would certainly be able to share the tasks, roles and expectations in the home more and more. If this were so, then we would start to see real balance and equality between the genders. However, a lot needs to change in the meantime. Men need to learn that women are there to stay in the workplace and have just as much to offer in any role. Women need to be willing to give up more of the decision making and primary care giving role in the household.

Currently society is not helping the gender balance debate at all. In most countries, it is a guarantee that the courts/state assumes and then legislates that the mother will always be the ultimate care giver of the children in a family. Therefore, men always feel secondary in the role of the family. Just like women were ill treated for so long by being ostracised from the workplace, men, too are often ostracised whenever the relationship breaks down between them and their partner. It is often very hard for them to gain equal access to their children. Sole custody tends to be a common outcome from many court systems and invariably the winner of that will tend to be the mother (approximately 80% of the time). Of course, the fact that sole custody, with limited visitation rights, is granted so liberally is a major bone of contention, as many worldwide studies show that neither men nor women should enjoy this privilege as a default. What should happen is that the best interests of the children should be taken into account. Invariably, this means that joint custody[2] should be the norm and standard.

If we want, and I believe we most definitely need, our men to be always active and fully engaged in the care, protection and rearing of their family, even if a marriage breaks down, then we have to afford them equal rights. However, it is very easy to point out all the men who have vacated their responsibilities over the centuries and walked out on their families. Legislators could use this as an argument as to why the state tends to make the provision for women to be the primary care giver. Obviously, then, more men need to evolve and step up to the mark and honour their responsibilities if they expect true equal rights in the family. Again, President Obama is particularly vociferous on this very topic, since it deals directly with individual responsibility.

"But if we are honest with ourselves, we'll admit that what too many fathers also are is missing - missing from too many lives and too many homes. They have abandoned their responsibilities, acting like boys instead of men. And the foundations of our families are weaker because of it...

We need fathers to realize that responsibility does not end at conception. We need them to realize that what makes you a man is not the ability to have a child - it's the courage to raise one[3]".

\*\*\*

Both sexes will never gain parity if neither will yield on key issues. The future could be very good indeed if both gave a little, to gain an awful lot more.

\*\*\*

## Summary

**Current Society:**
- Role of men fixed for most part as being in the role of worker only.

- Major public debate raging as to the role of women, i.e. balancing work life and home life.

**Sustainable Community:**

- Roles of both men and women involving a share of both duties, i.e. working and home based family duties.
- Reduced working week (as per earlier chapters) enables this joint endeavour.

# Nine: Losing Our Youth

One of the horrible things people in life people have to deal with is suicide. Unfortunately, it is most prevalent among the young, especially among young males ages 18-24. This is a very complex situation and one in which the families of those involved have years of anguish, turmoil and guilt to deal with over the subsequent decades. The one person who can answer the questions they have is the very one who is no longer around.

Is there any way we can stem the tide of this epidemic? Well, if we look at the issues we addressed in looking at educating our youth, maybe there are some things that can help. I think everyone would agree that one common thread in suicide is that people get isolated from those around them, and then this isolation sets in deeper and deeper. Finally, they lose perspective on their situation and the worst case scenario can ensue. The poor families of these people often put themselves through the wringer for years, berating themselves for not noticing the "signs".

However, we, as a wider society, also have a duty to these young people. If we had true sustainable education where we valued each and every child equally in society, we would also value their unique skills and contributions. Instead, we have a competitive learning environment where children often feel at a loss outside the home, where they feel insecure, and like they are being pitted against each other for the spoils of life.

Sometimes, it takes an outsider to notice when balance or perspective has been lost in an individual. Those nearest to a person cannot see those subtle signs of despair. If we were to adopt a plan where some older people in the community engaged with young people during the tender years of 14-18, as described in the sustainable education chapter, then they would act as gentle guides for the rocky road to young adulthood. It is no secret that people tend to become happier and more settled as they mature (once their basic needs are met), and so people in their sixties and seventies, who currently have no role in our society, could be perfect mentors for our youth. They have gotten over all the travails and pitfalls on their own journey, and very often know when to say the right thing, or intervene when gentle encouragement is needed. However, we are ignoring the needs of both the young and the old by not allowing this natural bonding take place.

The generations in the middle, i.e. the parents, are very often the people who are not needed by teenagers. Teenagers already tend to have validation from their parents (unfortunately not always), but what they are looking for is validation from society. They want to feel like they belong and that their life will mean something.

By giving them the space to explore their world and their emotions, hopefully we could find that these young people have more balance in their lives and so never get into a spiral of despair.

***

## Summary

**Current Society:**
- Teenagers often left to fend for themselves and hence tend to drift. Sullenness is a common trait of this age bracket, coupled with the bottling up of emotions and problems. If they become too isolated it can lead to a cycle of despair.
- Family often feel helpless to break through to teenagers. The happy go lucky child has turned into a not too pleasant person.

**Sustainable Community:**
- Mentoring and gentle guidance from community members, especially elderly non – judgemental people.
- Space given in education system for youth to find their voice.
- Sharing of emotions encouraged from a young age.
- Recognition that very often family is not needed to assist teenagers. Very often outside validation from other adults is needed.

## Ten: What is a Green Consumerist Bubble?

We are being preached at continuously that we are ruining the planet by our daily actions. It has been decided that the amount of $CO_2$ emissions in our atmosphere is in direct correlation with an increase in global average temperatures. One would need to have been on Mars for the last ten years to have missed out on this news story.

It may sound like I am being cynical, or doubting from my opening paragraph, but that is not the case. I fully support a move to less consumption in our society and to us all leading more sustainable lives. However, I strongly fear that we are being lined up for a fresh wave of consumerism wearing the guise of "going green".

We all witnessed the birthing, in the mid 1990's, of the internet. It is amazing that fifteen years ago, the internet was still in its infancy. In the five short years from 1995 to the turn of the century, we witnessed a huge surge of new companies, new technology and new careers in the areas of software development and any discipline related to computers. This was the positive aspect of it. The negative side was the fortunes gambled and lost; the get rich quick schemes and the belief that this exciting new industry was a licence to print money because there would always be a sucker who would buy one's product.

In 2000 everything came crashing down[1]. The emperor was shown to have no clothes and hundreds and thousands of new start up companies and existing businesses went under. The bubble burst. The secret was out. Companies with hugely inflated stock values who had never turned a profit were exposed and went under. This earthquake did not really hit the wider world, like the crash we are currently living through. Most people who lost their money in 2000 tended to be younger professionals who had access to the internet and knew about the inner workings of this world. For most other people in 2000, the internet and all associated companies were still a foreign country.

We survived that mini recession and then the great bubble of 2004-2008 happened world wide. A lot of people who lost money in the dotcom boom didn't learn their lesson and piled in again. This time, the bubble was property and cheap credit. It was a classic example of over extending and investing in areas that people did not understand. When confidence left, the market crashed. As sure as night follows day, we will survive this crash. However, the big fear is have we learnt our lesson this time?

If we don't move to a sustainable economy then we will not learn our lesson. We will lick our wounds for a few years and come 2012 or so, people will be looking for the next big thing to invest in. The "green" movement will be that thing. Already legislation changes around the world designed to make the world a greener place are having less than the desired outcome. Something is becoming greener alright; but thus far, it is just big business amassing more green backs than any saving of the world.

Carbon credits[2] are a classic example of this. Governments issued carbon credits to businesses to try and limit, and to ultimately reduce, the amount of $CO_2$ (and other Greenhouse gas emissions) in the atmosphere. Depending on the type and size of industry, more or less credits were issued. A market place was created whereby these credits could be sold to companies who had exceeded their quota by companies who didn't meet their own quota. Also, any carbon reducing or mitigating projects that were developed automatically generated fresh credits that could be traded. This meant companies could finance projects, especially in third world countries, and generate credits to use or trade themselves. However, as with any system, there were inherent flaws in setting up and administrating these schemes. No guarantee of long term reductions in Greenhouse gas emissions has been seen to date, and transparency is also a big problem. This is especially true of the practice of companies "investing" in projects in third world countries that have very long life cycles before they are operational (e.g. afforestation) and may not actually ever achieve their goal. However, carbon credits are issued on the back of these potentials.

Governments are now legislating to prevent all types of carbon dioxide emissions, be it from our homes or our transport. Schemes are being set up to quantify all of these emission levels[3]. One has to assume that carbon taxing for the individual will be as prevalent as income tax worldwide in a few short years. This is amazing. We are going to have a whole new classification of tax without yet having hard and definite proof that reducing carbon dioxide emissions will actually reverse or arrest global climate change.

Now, as stated, I am all for living less consumerist, more sustainable lifestyles which will *automatically* reduce carbon dioxide emissions as a direct consequence. But, to buy in to wholesale carbon taxing seems ludicrous to me. It seems so crazy because I know how inefficient big government is, how ill equipped it is to actually complete what it says it will do and ultimately how any form of carbon taxing will be a failure if handled this way. The notion of the "polluter pays" will be sold as a panacea to soothe people in this transition, but the burden will transfer to the individual and not to big business. It is easier to get money out of individual households than tackle vested interest in large business.

If at least some of the energy and money that will be poured into implementing costly initiatives to halt carbon emissions was put into setting up true sustainable communities worldwide, we would not only drastically reduce these emissions, but we would have a much healthier and more balanced world. If government invested in sustainable public transport, approved of and made bartering systems tax exempt, aided in sustainable education models and truly assisted people endeavouring to decouple from the current unsustainable economic model, then we would be in a much better position. That is just the governmental/legislative side of the green economy.

In the private sector, it seems like every single product in the marketplace has suddenly had a make over and is now referred to as "sustainable" or "green". In some cases, they have tried to make cosmetic changes to make the statement true, but in a lot more cases it is just a re-brand with absolutely no changes to the product, compared to how it was a few years ago. Of course, that does not help the business that has gone to great lengths and cost to truly make their product one that is minimising any damage to the earth. Of course, there are genuine people out there who truly want to marry a desire to be good for the environment with a business goal. That is commendable.

People will learn pretty quickly, though, that there is going to be (and are already) a lot of charlatans in the green industry.

The concept of buying even more products, to either reduce the impact of the products we already have or, indeed, to replace those products is a very questionable one. We do not know the life cycle in most cases of the products we are buying.

By this I mean that while a product may claim to reduce carbon dioxide emissions over existing products in the market place, we do not know for sure how much energy was expended in making this new product. Perhaps new raw materials were used in its manufacture that are far more damaging to the environment than the product it is replacing. That is why the whole drive to reduce carbon dioxide emissions is such a scary concept when taken on its own in isolation. It can very easily lead to the opposite, an increase in those self same emissions, or indeed, to far greater levels of pollution elsewhere.

It is far more effective to just get sensible about the consumption of things like electricity and water with the products we use today, than to trust private business to bring out whole new suites of products that are *definitely* better for the environment overall.

Very simple and effective changes can be implemented at the personal level. Again, if we strive for personal empowerment we take our power back from those who would exploit it.

Domestically, we can collect rain water[4]. If water charges are not already in your town, city or country, they are not far away. Collect rain water and get it plumbed into your toilets and washing machine. This is a simple and cost effective way to recycle water, reduce your ongoing charges, and reduce the amount of water treatment needed by public authorities as less "clean water" is needed for these purposes.

Become aware of your consumption of electricity. Appliances are rated for energy consumption in watts. Utility companies charge us in something called kWh, kilo watt hours. 1000 watts consumption for 1 hour equals 1kWh. So if you had an appliance that runs for 1 hour at 1000 watt consumption it is costing you a kWh. Depending on your country, or indeed, locality you will be charged different tariffs for a kWh. Also, kWhs are cheaper at night, generally, as there is not so much demand for electricity then.

With this little knowledge, one can ascertain, for example, that things like tumble dryers or electric ovens, or the humble electric kettle (2-3kW) are big consumers of energy. Therefore, attack your consumption of these high wattage products. Become more efficient at managing the running of these. For example, most clothes will dry better and more naturally outdoors. Just use a tumble dryer for a 10 minute final dry instead of the whole drying process.

Conversely, charging a mobile phone or using low energy lighting (10-20W) are cheap consumers of energy. It makes sense to understand what the high consumers are. Then, if one is to make decisions on new purchases to reduce energy consumption, go after the heavy hitters. It doesn't make sense to buy some new "green" phone that may be saving just a few watts of power over an older one when one is still wasting needless energy on drying all clothes in a tumble dryer.

Become very discerning about the products being marketed to you with green credentials. A few very basic questions to the sales person will highlight pretty quickly if it does what it says on the tin. If it claims that it will be 20% more efficient that existing products, then look for proof or independent verification of same. Ask what materials are involved in the make up, what is their company's policy on recycling, how they handle their waste, where do they source their electricity from, etc. All of these questions let them know you are a discerning purchaser who does care about the environment and will not buy into any statement without proof.

***

## Summary

**Current Society:**
- Green is the new mantra. Purchasing green products, building green, investing in green businesses, jobs in green industries. It is seen as a cure to many ills.

**Sustainable Community:**
- All of the green agenda is standard fare but comes with a strong health warning. People not duped into consuming unnecessarily to become "green".

# Eleven: Spirituality

Many have died over the millennia for the concept of religion and spirituality. For some reason, the very part of our lives that is supposed to provide guidance to us on how to lead healthy and wholesome lives, where we honour ourselves and our neighbour, is the very area that often promotes the most conflict.

From what I have seen of all the world's main religions, they all have one thing in common. The original message[1] speaks about the concept of personal empowerment, of owning up to our roles in life, of taking on the mantle of our own power. We are assured that if we do this, then we will find peace in our own hearts. Following on from this, if we are to find peace in our own hearts, it makes sense we will not perpetrate ills on others or on those in weaker positions than us.

I believe the reason people engage so strongly in religion is that they are desperately seeking community. The strongest sense of community is often that formed around a religion. If we are active members of a faith, we will attend worship (with other people), we will celebrate the rituals of life and death in this faith (with other people), and we will align our beliefs with those of the faith (with other people). The common thread is the desire to form community with other people.

So why do we seem to be still trapped in desperate conflict situations around the world where religion is often the main cause of the conflict?

I don't believe there are inherent problems with either attending worship or celebrating rituals in the faith of our choosing. I believe the problems arise when we give up our power and align our beliefs totally with those of the faith. Because people are so keen on the feeling of kinship and community, this then is the very thing that is used exploitatively by people in power. Religion is used as the vehicle to promote hidden agendas. The original message of the faith, around personal empowerment and care for one another and the world, can and does get corrupted.

This is where the absolute truth that was first laid down, that gave people the keys and the knowledge on how to free themselves from turmoil to gain personal power, have ended up being corrupted by human hands in the intervening time. These human hands use sections of doctrine in isolation, or twist the original meaning of the faith to meet their own needs. Then, since the people want nothing more than to feel the security and kinship of community within the faith, they go along willingly with the altered doctrines that only serve selfish needs and do not meet the needs of the people.

People have been recruited throughout history into armies to "defend the faith". It was never to defend the faith, for the faith does not need defending. It was to defend the selfish interests of man that these wars have been waged. How can a faith need defending when it is absolute truth. It gives man on earth all the tools necessary to lead good, wholesome, powerful lives. All religions have this central thread running through them as the original message, that of a key to empower oneself and the world around oneself.

We have seen the turning away from all religions by many people. Some have very strongly come out and said they cannot believe in any God or spiritual force when all one needs to do is look at the carnage carried out in the name of that God. They have a valid point and deserve credit for making a stand like that. However, one also needs to realise that by stating such a thing, it aligns them into their own community too; the community of the non-believer who share similar ideas. Again, one has to wonder if the desire to not believe is at the same time a calling out for a sense of community.

I am not going to name individual religions, or even non-believing groups, or discuss pros and cons of their belief systems and who I feel has the most claims on being the true faith. I believe we all are entitled to our viewpoint of the world and our connection with whatever greater force, if any, we believe in.

However, what I will say is that humanity all share a bond to be in proper alignment and community with each other. When we have full support around us from people who we care about, our problems never seem too big.

\*\*\*

## What are some of the keys laid down in original format to empower people?

- We were told to find quiet time. To truly sit and find a contemplative period in every day to let our natural wisdom rise to the surface. Remember, if everything is of the earth, then so are we. Our bodies are made of the earth, the earth sustains us and we have the wisdom of its history coursing through us. It has the answers to everything. If we sit and find space she will share those answers with us.
- We have infinite power. It is not being powerless that people fear, but the opposite. To have power or be powerful in life presents decisions and opportunities for growth that many wish to shy away from.
- If we embrace our power, it will not lead to abuse. For anyone who truly embraces the power of their hearts will only direct it for good in the world. People who commit crimes and ill against others are not powerful; they are coming from a position of weakness.
- We can handle any situation that arises in our lives. We can process the negativity and hand it to the earth for purification. We do not have to hold onto ills perpetrated against us forever. We can be free in heart and body.
- We are meant to lead passionate lives. We are meant to be joyful every day, to have the surety of purpose and enthusiasm for life to embrace it fully.
- We are meant to be creative beings that create beauty on earth. The idea of a Garden of Eden is not meant for the after life only. We can, and need to create our own Garden of Eden on earth today. We are expected to build our own **cities of gold**. It is why man has free will; to design and choose, alter, agree and disagree and ultimately reach a point where we can all contribute to the creation of a better world.

This is the key to forming sustainable community in the world. If we can take our power back from religions, from government or from institutions that are failing us, we can and will move into a much safer, more prosperous, and healthier future. This doesn't mean that we end up with millions of despots running around who suddenly feel all "powerful". Quite the opposite. If everyone takes the time in their lives to find their true voice, then that voice will prompt them into a cycle of enormous change that will only serve to empower and give meaning to their lives.

This is already happening without people's consent. So many people are having the rug pulled out from under them by events they feel are outside of their making. In the process, they are finding alternative paths, other than the well trodden mainstream ones and finding that far from those new paths alienating them, they in fact, dovetail beautifully with people of similar minds and lead to a new sense of community.

***

## Summary

**Current Society Spirituality:**
- Dogmatic belief that all other religions bar the one we follow are inherently flawed or wrong.
- Gross corruption of the original message of the religion by man.
- Exploitation of people to follow certain dogmatic practices based on their desire to be in community.
- Religions having too great a role in educational facilities and politics world wide.
- No historical legacy of a reverence and respect for the earth that nurtures humanity. (Feminine energy ignored for millennia). This has contributed to exploitation of the earth by mankind.

**Sustainable Community Spirituality:**
- Allow space for individual to find their own relationship (or not) with a greater force.
- Sense of community is generated by the actual community day to day, so the desire to form community only through a religion is superseded.

- Religions now revert to the teaching and practising of the original message, namely that of love for self, fellow man and the earth.
- Puts reverence and respect for the earth as a cornerstone of society.
- Acknowledgement that all resources we use and everything we need for life comes from the earth.

# Twelve: Democracy

It is a fact that in the western style democracies, millions of people lead a safe, protected and relatively prosperous life. Note, I did not mention that it affords them happy lives as a consequence, or indeed prosperous lives for all, but overall, the system has many benefits.

The place we came from in the western world to the point of widespread democracy was a bloody and harsh world. The people were mainly the play things of feudal landlords, local monarchies, or tyrannical leaders. They were often the fodder that provided the wealth from the bottom up through unjust taxes and exploitation. They were also the foot soldiers for wars of vanity and greed. It was a system of slavery in all but name. Unfortunately, there are still many, many places in the world where this gross exploitation of people is happening.

Luckily, here in the western world we have gone through much of this grief and pain (which culminated with WW11) and have demanded through the centuries the rights to live our lives in relative peace and prosperity. This is democracy as we know it. We all get the right to vote at the point of maturation; eighteen years of age in most countries. The noble concept being that we elect a representative who will be a voice for us individually, especially when it comes to regional or national issues that affect our lives.

Unfortunately, it is from this point on that the problems start. The business end of administering democracy has become inept, corrupt, and is so far removed from the daily lives of people that they feel totally disconnected and disenfranchised.

One of the main reasons for this is the party political system. Be they democratic, republican, socialist, labour movements, Christian leaning or of the green persuasion, all party politics becomes a business in itself. It is run like a company with a leader or CEO, senior executives, middle managers and foot soldiers. Loyalty to the party brand is of paramount importance, more so than loyalty to the individual.

The idea of governance from the bottom up, (the way it should be) is thrown out the window. Instead, we get governance from the top down, regardless of the individual who enables and votes for the system and politicians in the first place. That is the absolute irony. Once every political term, however long it is in each country, these politicians canvass, beg, plead and often make us feel afraid of the alternatives if we do not vote for them and put them back into power. We, the electorate, hold all the power in these elections. However, it is for such a short time span that we hold this power, in reality only a matter of weeks during a campaign. Then, once these politicians are elected, they hold all the aces again until the next time they call to you, the individual, for a vote.

In the interim, are they working for you?

The sad reality is that in nearly all cases they are not. It is not that they are bad or evil people, but those they work for in this period are often those that shout the loudest and make the most waves. So often this is big business, which has tremendous lobbying power and influence of governments' world wide. They will spend vast sums of money to influence, in whatever way they can, the shaping of legislation that will directly affect their business.

Also, the other master of the elected representative is their alliance to the political party to which they are aligned. They cannot, and do not, have the individual as their priority when they are voting with their party just to defeat an opposition party. Above all else, their main desire is not to destabilise their positions while in governance and so a split in their camps, whereby individual politicians vote with their morals or with their constituents, is not tolerated.

Therefore it is not democracy as it should be. Your voice is not getting heard, unless your voice is the one that can lobby and influence the corridors of power.

Finally, there is tremendous wasting of resources in western democracies. By the nature of governance, layers upon layers of bureaucracy are set up, very often to insulate those in power from being held accountable for decision making. They are so terrified of making mistakes that, very often, many different groups, sub groups, committees and advisors are employed to make accountability impossible. This culture then spreads like a cancer through all public representative bodies to the point where we have gross wastage of tax incomes and where severe incompetence is acceptable. The people who work in these systems despair at their inability to streamline or make them efficient, and then often give up trying.

Democracy from the top down, (while starting out as a noble concept in nearly all cases) so often ends up being inefficient, incompetent, disconnected and totally unsuitable to meet the needs of the individual people on the ground.

**So what should democracy be?**

I believe democracy should start in the home. As outlined in the earlier chapters, there needs to be democracy between the sexes in the home, i.e. an equality of roles in both family and working life. We also need to listen to the needs of our children. By that I mean affording them a true sustainable education where their unique talents, career desires and skill sets will become apparent to them and us. That is democracy, giving a true voice to the young who are unable to vote.

We need to extend equal rights to the elderly in our communities, by allowing them to contribute their lifetime of knowledge and skills back to the community if they so wish.

Once democracy is successful in the home, then it is also successful in our immediate community. The examples listed of affording democracy to three subsets of our population, namely children, adults and older citizens straight away spills into our local community as we need the assistance of those outside the four walls of our home to enable them.

The point is we are being democratic in our daily lives. Then, if we evolve to the point of embodying true sustainable communities where we have concepts like bartering, building of communal business/recreational buildings and shared food production, then we are applying the principle of democracy we learned in the home to the running of the community. That principle is true respect for the voices of all the individuals.

**So where does the current party political system that dominates our democracies fit in with this concept?**

In a similar way that cash has become too dominant in our economy, party politics has become too dominant a force in our lives. If we were to embody a lot of the principles outlined above for democracy in our immediate community, then we are starting to take our individual power away from politicians and political groupings.

They say all politics is local. If this is true then we, the individual people, should be deciding our future at a local level, i.e. at the community level of 150 people or less. If we can run a community of this size democratically, then we do not need legislation from the top down to run the minutiae of our lives.

People today are far too passive and will accept any legislation, ruling or directive that filters down from the ruling classes. They feel disengaged, isolated, disenfranchised and obsolete. If these same people started to actively make decisions about how their immediate environment and community should run, then it takes back a lot of that lost power.

In time, if this model of active citizenship flourished, we would find that so much of the power we hand over willingly to the national political systems would be wiped out as a natural consequence. I am not advocating abolishing the current system in its entirety. However, it needs to play a far smaller role, albeit an important one, in the running of our countries and world.

Their role should be confined to larger issues relating to the long term direction and running of a country, i.e. to implement ten year, fifty year and one hundred year sustainable national plans. Their job should be to work with other nations to align with their visions and plans so we can generate a long term sustainable plan for the world and for our human society.

Most importantly of all, their job should be to enable sustainable democracy among the people NOW, while they hold the power. They need to start promoting and supporting bartering systems, to deregulate education to allow for more holistic models, to support active retirement for people and to stop wasting resources on inefficient governance.

***

Many people would argue that an active citizenship democratic model could never work in reality. California is an example of a place where this type of policy has been running and, in many ways, it is fair to classify it as a failure. This state has allowed direct democracy to work side by side with representative democracy since 1911. The noble intention is that it can give the people on the street a direct say in the running of the state. What has happened over the years is that many special interest groups have hijacked the system and used it to push through their own particular pet projects.

I believe the problem in that state, and others, is that their model is still fitting in with the existing structures of governance found elsewhere in the world. Therefore, it is not coming from a position of true individual empowerment where people are solving their own problems together at a local level first, before trying to influence broader state wide issues. Instead, it is coming from people who are obviously unhappy with their current society and are using this vehicle to try and change their futures. It will never be successful until it is combined with both personal empowerment (to not abuse the system) and until the voices are coming from strong local communities working effectively side by side.

***

My proposals for a more sustainable economy, allowing for bartering, etc. to the detriment of the current existing systems, are workable. Let's look at the situation today where people work long hard hours to pay for the taxes, goods and services that are needed to survive in life. So much of the taxes they pay are wasted! Literally, they are washed away in a bureaucratic morass. We pay taxes for high standards of necessities like infrastructure, healthcare and education, and yet we turn out millions of semi-illiterate people from our schools annually. Obviously, the system is failing them. We have hugely discredited health care systems and similar catastrophes in our infrastructures (e.g. waste, sewage and road problems).

If government played less of a part in our daily lives, coupled with us being able to streamline public services, it would mean we would have to pay far less taxes. Instead, we are currently pouring tax revenue into trying to sustain the unsustainable. If we are paying less taxes, it means we are working less, perhaps going back to the four hour working day, or we are involved in bartering and trading our services to sustain ourselves.

We still need government, as mentioned, for areas like national development plans and for large scale infrastructure. But, this government model requires the current one to rapidly evolve to meet our needs.

***

One major issue of the future that people will need to learn to overcome is NIMBYism, i.e. the mentality that you can build it anywhere, but **Not In My Back Yard.** If we end up with empowered individuals running local communities, coupled with a devolved less powerful national executive charged with only large scale national interest planning, then it will make sense that at some point, potential conflict may arise between the two. If the national executive decides a country needs a particular piece of infrastructure that will improve the lives of a major proportion of people, then the local communities this directly impacts will need to learn to adapt. Of course, this is only when the change is a last resort and is definitely the best solution. So often in our society we see large scale infrastructure being implemented that is neither for the greater good, nor indeed, logical in anyway. Its implementation is often due to intense lobbying, or due to an administration refusing "to lose face" by admitting their policy was incorrect in the first instance.

Once we have determined something is for the greater good and does need to disrupt a minority to serve the majority, then we need to collectively reach compromise. Alternative arrangements will need to be made, beyond the obvious one of financial compensation, to help enable these people to either adjust to changed circumstances in their current locality, or to adjust to a new environment. We need to learn to put the collective interest ahead of self serving interests once change like above is warranted and needed by a majority of people.

***

If we can have less top down policy driven governance and more bottom up people centred improvements of lives, then I believe there can be a meeting place in the middle where government and the people can be mutually beneficial.

**In essence, we the people need to step up to the mark and current governments need to step down from their ivory towers.** The people who will run this streamlined government of the future will need to be more in tune with the people they represent, but also will need to be visionaries for where the world should go and where the evolution of our species should aim for.

In truth, these people will most likely evolve naturally out of the sustainable community model itself, where they have learned the basics of self empowerment, healthy community governance, and have a desire and passion to link the goals of small individual communities to those of hundreds and thousands of other communities nationally and internationally. Then, they truly will be of the people and for the people and perhaps this wonderful institution called democracy could work effectively for all people.

***

## Summary

### Current Society Democracy:
- Biggest lobbyists get the ear of the politician.
- Party politics defines political voting pattern.
- Gross inefficiencies in public services and infrastructure.
- Losses of accountability as decisions filter down and get implemented.
- Major disillusionment in public sector workers and in the

public in general.
- Governments fire fight daily. Very poor at implementing medium and long term plans for society.
- Top down governance.

**Sustainable Community Democracy:**
- Households run democratically, respecting voices of all ages.
- Local community run democratically to fix local problems and plan for the future. This breeds skilled people who can engage with other sustainable communities.
- Less need for state control of all public services as local communities efficiently resolve their own local issues.
- Smaller public sector needed to deal with local issues.
- People own their local problems; hence they cannot blame governance anymore. Local community dealing with local issues.
- Government now only needed for long term planning of bigger issues, like society development, and country to country negotiations.
- Government office holders of the future will come from sustainable community model.
- Bottom up governance.

# Thirteen:  Role of Communicative Technology

The telephone, television and the internet have been three of the most fascinating and brilliant inventions of our world. In essence, if we look at the three of these technologies, what they are doing is putting people in communion with each other, aside from the obvious role of entertainment. Once again, one of our most basic needs is to feel part of a grouping of people, to feel like our life has meaning and that we are needed.

These technologies perform the virtual connection that allow people feel they are in community. However, while this is a good thing it unfortunately misses the one vital ingredient, i.e. that ability to allow people feel the actual physical presence of the groupings they desire. There is a detachment to them that does not bridge that need for human contact.

We have evolved as a society away from the community. As populations increased and people moved in larger numbers to cities and suburbs, housing needs were often met by the building of apartments or housing estates. Instead of helping to build community, these housing solutions often isolated people. The advent of technologies like those listed above have helped people to get more and more subsumed into the lifestyle of isolation in their homes. So often somebody returns from work tired, and then proceeds to spend all their spare time being passive receptors of information from technology, especially in the format of television and the internet.

Life would feel so much more worthwhile if we could reconnect with like minded people and have common goals and desires that improved our own lives and those of our locality. Often, people are afraid to engage with their immediate environment and their community. It is a fear of possible confrontation and disagreement that prevents them from making the leap. Disagreement and subsequent compromise are what are so fascinating about the human condition. It is inevitable conflict will arise, but the healthy resolution of that conflict is a wonderful thing. It also explains why the few end up running our local governance and communities, those that are not afraid to "put themselves out there". We all need to step up to the mark to engage with each other and break down the walls of isolation.

In that context, communicative devices and technology are wonderful, but are the crutches we rely on to feel part of society. There is a big irony in people communicating online so eloquently with others of a similar mind, but failing to speak to, or engage with people in public. It doesn't make sense. Ultimately, technology will never meet that basic human desire for connection.

It does, however, act as a fantastic resource for our education and for the proliferation of ideas and movements worldwide. Nothing of significance can happen in the world without us all knowing about it within minutes or hours, not days or weeks as before.

The proliferation of modern technologies is also acting as a conduit to disseminate a lot of information of evil that was perpetrated against people worldwide, both historically and currently. A lot of skeletons are getting aired with the advent of communications technology, again a necessary step to the gaining of personal power in the world.

Without doubt, we will be bombarded by more efficient, complex, fascinating and exciting technologies in the coming years. They will be marketed, as always, as being the holy grail of consumption with so much capacity, so many features, and so many cool gadgets. Unfortunately, nothing will ever compare to sharing our joys, success and problems with people around us who are also looking for meaning and purpose in their own lives.

In truth it is like we will come full circle. Our ancestors had an intimate knowledge of their immediate locality and community, but lacked knowledge of the outside world. We could easily return to the idea of community to enrich our lives like they did, but the advantage we have is the ready access to modern technology to let us see what is happening in the outside world and to keep abreast of changes. A mixing of both would provide a nice balance.

# Fourteen:  Healthy Body and Mind

Arguably, the most important thing in the world for a person is to have a healthy mind and body. It is only with the loss of health that we realise what a precious gift it is. Something like a weekend of toothache, waiting for a dentist to open on a Monday morning, is the only time healthy people get to realise what life must be like for those whose lives are dominated by a disease or disability. The good news for that person is that short term pain like this will get fixed and their lives can revert to normal quite quickly.

It is something that is priceless; the ability to live mostly pain and disease free right through to old age. We are lucky if this is the case. If we have our health, it is often very hard to empathise with those who do not.

Technology has brought tremendous success to the treatment of, and curing of diseases. Surgery has advanced light years in terms of its complexity and intricateness and the surgical procedures now available are simply mind boggling. We owe a great debt of gratitude to science, doctors and engineers who are constantly evolving these technologies and procedures to enable more and more people to become pain free, disease free and healthy in their lives. It is fantastic that life spans are increasing all the time, (another reason why population growth is increasing) and the risk of early death drops all the time.

People nowadays are not so deferential to their medical consultants, and with the advent of the internet, are able to research any conditions that they acquire and so are able to take an active part in their own treatment process. This gives them a tremendous sense of empowerment.

While all of the above is fantastic, it must be noted that a lot of it is at the point of disease being in place, or where surgery is required. We are not so good at taking the power in our hands to ensure disease does not set in, in the first place. Like I mentioned, it is only when we have pain that we realise how fortunate we are that we do not live like this all the time.

***

Diet is a crucial part of our health. If we eat good, healthy and natural foods, we will not suffer from so many of the endemic diseases of today that stem from a great crisis facing our population and individual health; that being worldwide rising obesity levels.

People assume that the products and foods in their lives are benign in nature. In only the last fifty years or so has large scale manufactured food been part of our lives. Up to that point, we ate locally grown organic foods that had a very traceable path from the earth to our tables. Nowadays, we eat imported foods from all over the world and also consume a huge variety of processed foods. By doing this, we do not have control over the content or true quality of this food. While the food may meet government standards in terms of preparation and hygiene, we have to understand these foods are often specifically manufactured to taste good. If something is specifically manufactured to taste good, then one has to question what is in it to do this. If we look at it in the most basic terms, then sugar is definitely one of the nicest and sweet tasting foodstuffs in the world. So much of manufactured food is filled with sugar or sugar tasting products.

Long term consumption of too much sugar leads to a thickening of the waist area and the gaining of unhealthy levels of weight. As organs lay down layers of fat, they become more and more at risk of becoming unhealthy and ultimately diseased. That is why diabetes and heart disease, etc. arise from years of intake of unsuitable foodstuffs that lead to a sharp rise in weight gain and a weakening of the body's defence mechanisms.

If we reverted to a more natural and even keeled food intake that did not include so much sugar based foods, we would reduce dramatic weight gain in our lives. One of the problems with diets is that they often do not highlight the foodstuffs that are actually making people heavier. People believe that relatively large quantities of breads, pastas, rice and potatoes should form a central part of their diet, and indeed, be the filler in all meals. However, these foodstuffs, while fine in moderation, are actually some of the worst for weight gain, in that they turn into sugar through digestion. If we eat large quantities of the complex carbohydrates[1] that comprise these foods, all the training or other dieting in the world will not help us to lose weight. It is why so many people train and diet and yet fail to lose any weight. Very often their diets are targeting the wrong areas of consumption.

It all comes back again to people taking the power back into their own lives to create healthy bodies for themselves. Millions, and indeed over 33 billion dollars in the USA annually is spent in trying to lose weight by people worldwide. They are all seeking that one magic tablet or method that will enable them to lose weight. They do not realise that the key to losing weight is to take all the power back from outside sources and to envision that future for oneself and then eating a balanced healthy diet to attain it. Envisioning means seeing oneself at the ideal healthy weight that is best suited for that individual. Act as if that weight target has been achieved, or is in the process of being achieved. Either way, one builds a picture of oneself at this weight and sensible choices can start to be made in the moment regarding food and its effect on that vision.

The lack of awareness around what food is good, and what is bad, is a major downfall; people often cutting out anything with fat in it, but the irony is that often fat will not put on weight directly. Very often, it is foodstuffs that turn into sugar through digestion that put on weight, and very often that is the foodstuffs we innocently increase consumption of while we diet from other foods. I am not advocating a full fat only diet, far from it, but I am advising a balanced diet where some knowledge is known about the long term effects of excessive complex carbohydrate consumption. Hopefully, people will not load up on these foodstuffs while they diet from other foodstuffs and end up perpetuating the cycle of unhealthy weight gain.

We can also take more power back over what we eat by growing our own foods. Very often it may not be practical to do so for one individual family, i.e. a lot of fresh produce could be wasted and the individuals may not wish to grow their own. However, if we engage more and more with our communities, we can share food production, and get people with skills in food preparation, to transform them in to tasty and healthy foods for our tables. Again, if we had a barter type economy in our local community then the growing of food could be a unique role for one person (or a few people), while the transformation of the food into tasty meals for the tables of the community could be a role for another person (or a few people). These would be skills and services that they would offer as trades for others in the community to offset against goods and services they could avail of themselves elsewhere.

*** 

Another area that leads to problems, and ultimately disease in our lives, is our mental health. Our society has become very isolating, and we fail to realise that there are millions of people worldwide living lives of quiet desperation. For those with a physical condition, it is easier to label it and get the required treatment. However, there are many people who are suffering a gloomy malaise in their lives, or who are even suffering from a huge sense of depression.

Society is far less tolerant of those people. Any "dis-ease" of the mind is considered a major weakness by our society. The economic, educational and consumerist society we have created is meant to be the desire of all its citizens. Unfortunately, this is far from the truth. There are millions and millions of people who have no interest in amassing wealth or consuming goods and services, ad nausea. They want to lead lives that mean something; they wish to feel part of their community and to inspire and lead the way for their children and grandchildren.

When these basic needs are not met, it can lead ultimately to depression. Since depression is so taboo in our society, it is often not recognised by the individual and so the body can manifest[2] the "dis-ease" into any number of secondary physical ailments. I contend, certainly, that among the elderly that this could be true. The human has amazing will and if an elderly person feels isolated, lonely, and of no use, this desperation in their lives and minds could possibly manifest into the serious illnesses so common to their age bracket. I know many people would rubbish this suggestion, but those elderly people who live active lives, where they feel connected to, and useful in society, often have much greater levels of health and longevity[3].

It ties back into the concept of working less throughout our lives and then still having some energy and desire to contribute in old age. It gives those people a guaranteed role and function in society, and reduces the grip of depression and malaise. If these conditions cannot take a foothold in their lives, perhaps life threatening illnesses like cancer cannot find a similar foothold.

The same is true of the younger generations in our societies. We need to recognise the right of our youth to grow into the people they were meant to be, regardless of their subsequent career choice, sexual orientation or viewpoints. If we do this for them, then it prevents them feeling a desperate sense of isolation as they try to figure these things out on their own, and as they deal with the fallout if their choices do not fit the mainstream. Hopefully, we are winning the fight against depression and isolation, or suicidal tendencies, gaining a foothold with our youth as they traverse this volatile stage of their lives.

The more engaged we feel in our community, the more we feel the support of family and friends, the more we share life's joys and sorrows, and the more secure we feel in our ability to sustain ourselves and our families, means we are more likely to beat any "dis-ease" of the mind. Again, by engaging more, we take our power back in our health. If we take our power back in areas like our diet and our mental health, it will definitely lead to far less disease in our society and therefore we will not need the medical profession performing such heroics for our needs.

*** 

## Summary

### Current Society:
- Soaring obesity levels, leading to major crisis in the future with health related problems. This has to be tied in with move to consumption of cheap processed foods in the

past 50 years, coupled with more sedentary lifestyles.
- Mental health problems are huge in society.
- People often feel too isolated to even "own up" to their problems.
- Manifestation of mental health issues into physical ailments, especially in more vulnerable demographics.

**Sustainable Community:**
- More local production and "manufacture" of food. These will naturally be healthier as they will not be mass produced.
- Lifestyle more engaging as community works and plays together, hence people will cease to be so sedentary.
- Mental health problems, while still present, will have much less of a hold over people due to more and more active engagement in the community. We should see less knock on physical diseases as a result.

# Fifteen: Healthy Land

From an earlier chapter we saw that everything we do or use in life is of and from the earth. She sustains us and provides for us in our daily lives. We use her for shelter and avail of her resources. We claim ownership over parts of her body, but if we look beyond the surface of this claim, we know it is a crazy concept. How can we possibly own the earth considering its longevity and advanced intelligence. Again, the analogy of the mother entertaining the immaturity of her children springs back to mind. We are not all powerful over the earth.

While she offers us succour and shelter, it is also true that she does not want us to build on parts of her body. The earth has a complex magnetic system[1] spreading out over the entire globe. This magnetic system resonates and is in harmony with the frequency of living organisms like human beings. This is because all life has evolved from the earth while the magnetic field was already in place and so had to become compatible with it. This compatibility occurs at a frequency of 7.83 hertz (Hz). This is a measurable frequency and is known as the Schumann Resonance[2]. Long term exposure to this frequency is beneficial for us as humans and will generally lead to long and disease free lives. Unfortunately, problems arise with our health when we are exposed to distortions in its intensity. These distortions can arise from under the ground itself or can come from over the ground from man made constructions and technology.

First, let us look to the earth underneath us. Underground anomalies in the earths crust lead to an amplification of the magnetic field above ground to higher frequencies. Instead of the magnetic field operating at 7.83 Hz, it could now be operating at a frequency >100 Hz. If living organisms are exposed to these lines of distortion over a long period of time, it will ultimately lead to ill health. These anomalies may result from underground water streams, from fault lines or earthquakes. They can also evolve and shift over time.

The areas where these weak points exist are known as lines of geopathic stress[3](GS). Long term exposure to GS is not good for humans. We will always be exposed to GS lines as we go about our daily business. We will walk into an out of these lines without even realising it. That is unavoidable and is not a problem because the exposure is not prolonged. The problems arise if we are stationery in one location and a GS line is also in this spot. If sleeping in the path of these lines, people never get a full nights rest, often waking up lethargic and still tired. That is because their bodies' cells have not had a chance to rest and rejuvenate, as they are in a constant state of stress and anxiety due to the increased magnetic field they are being subjected to. Over time, if the body does not have a chance to rest and repair, then it dramatically weakens the immune system and it is at this point that serious illness can set in.

Information like this was common knowledge to our distant ancestors. They had an intuitive understanding of the earth that hosted them and knew her points of weakness. They never built on these weak points.

Unfortunately today, it is not the case that we do not build on lines of geopathic stress. Land is seen as a commodity and a means of generating great profit. Planners sit in city based offices and draw lines through maps based on political decisions to zone land as agricultural, industrial, commercial, green belt or residential. Obviously, for those who own land, they wish it to get zoned as residential or commercial/industrial as it is seen to be the most profitable and lucrative. People eventually end up purchasing or renting a home in a development that got rezoned as above. They need shelter for themselves and their families. However, a certain proportion of our housing could be built in part or in whole over areas of geopathic stress. Similarly, people could gain employment in a company and be required to sit at a particular desk in an office for forty hours a week. That particular desk may be right in the path of a line of GS and so its occupant will be adversely affected for years. The horrible irony is their colleague at the next desk could be out of the line of GS and so is suffering no ill effects.

Animals are very sensitive to geopathic stress and will not remain in an area of it if avoidable. Their bodies are sufficiently sensitive to know when they are discomforted and they take evasive action. The good news is that these lines are often only metres wide and so can be easily avoided. Therefore cattle, dogs and horses, as examples, will move out of an area of geopathic stress when they feel it. It explains why cattle may never occupy and rest in a corner or a part of a field they graze in. A problem arises when stables are built over a GS line. In that case, they become agitated and subsequently ill. As an aside, cats, ants, snakes and insects tend to love GS and often gravitate towards it. Unfortunately for them, while it is attractive in the short term, it is not good for their long term health. If a cat tends to curl up on a particular part of a bed or sofa repeatedly, it is a good sign that there is GS in that area.

We have become disconnected from our intuitive perceptions throughout the centuries and so lost the ability to "read" for lines of GS. Unlike the animals above, we fail to register that we are feeling lethargic, run down or just miserable. We often assume we just need a boost and drink a coffee or take some stimulant to "energise us", instead of realising our environment could be causing our symptoms.

We often do end up building our houses over these anomalies and, if we are unlucky enough to have our bed in the path of one, we could have years of discomfort and subsequent ill health. The scary thing is that it is a lottery; some people will buy houses with no geopathic stress, some will live in houses that have it in areas like bathrooms where it is not detrimental, while the unlucky ones live in homes where it passes through their bedrooms or living rooms where they spend nearly half their lives combined.

These houses either should not have been built in the first place, or the geopathic stress should have been corrected before it was built. Luckily, we can negate the effect of geopathic stress through several different techniques[4]. It can be detected quite easily by a dowser who will generally be able to provide a solution as well.

Again, awareness and empowerment is the key here. If we know about GS then we are aware it can lead to ill health. Therefore, we can get our homes checked to see if it is present. If it is there it can be fixed as above and hence we can see if the removal of the stress improves our health. There are only a few countries world wide that have integrated the correction of geopathic stress into their planning process; namely parts of Germany and Switzerland. They have performed sufficient research to satisfy themselves that it is a definite boost to human health if geopathic stress lines are eliminated.

Another problem causing emanation from the earth is radon gas. While it is does not affect the magnetic field of the earth it is still a problem for humans. It has been proven[5] to lead to the onset of lung cancer in humans. Radon will seep up through the foundations of a house from the earth and will get trapped in the structure of the house. Here it is absorbed by the body and again, over time, will lead to health problems. However, because radon gas emanations tend to be more concentrated in particular areas of the earth, its effects have been more noticeable over time than GS. Therefore, society and science have validated its effects on people and have implemented remedial fixes for it in building construction. Radon barriers are now integrated as standard practice in many countries that have high radon emissions from the ground, into the foundations of buildings.

Awareness of these issues is highly empowering. Radon reduction in our buildings is definitely considered more mainstream and as pointed out, is a science in itself. However, GS is a major problem in our world that is contributing greatly to ill health in our populations and it is time it became recognised by society. It is time we started to understand mother earth.

*** 

The second source of distortions to the life affirming magnetic field that sustains us comes from activities above ground. We need to gain more collective strength in blocking widespread and profligate dissemination of potentially harmful technologies like mobile phone transmitting stations, high voltage power lines, etc., until we have more solid proof that these are definitely not detrimental to human health.

These technologies emit high EMF's (electromagnetic fields) which can distort the natural frequency we find our peace and solace at of 7.83Hz. The more we are subjected to high levels of

EMF, the more susceptible our immune systems are to being worn down. If we take a walk in a wild area of nature, we often feel really refreshed and invigorated afterwards. The main reason for this is we have been subjected to an environment operating exclusively at a frequency of 7.83 Hz. Even if we passed through small areas of GS, we would not notice their effects because we are on the move. However, if we go to a city for a prolonged period of time, we can often feel drained and run down by just walking around. That is because that particular part of the earth's surface is subjected to a lot of distortions of the earth's magnetic field from all sorts of man made devices like underground power lines, transmitters, electronic devices, etc.

Very often technology like this is subjected to a standardised test to check its impact on human health. If it passes this test, then it is deemed safe for public consumption. However, our human bodies are the most sensitive instruments out there and if the installations of devices like these are causing problems for people, this should be the litmus test, regardless of standardised testing.

The home or place of work should be a place or nourishment, respite and rejuvenation. It is very unfair if that is the very place that is making us ill or contributing to ill health. We need to learn to be better readers of the land and ascertain both the positive and negative elements of our surroundings. It makes sense that in time, we should be evolving to a point where we centralise a lot of technology transmitters, etc. in areas of the earth's surface that are already "contaminated" by excessive activity underneath the earth's surface, i.e. from GS. We should then try to neutralise and heal the places where we have our buildings, be they homes or places of work, and make sure all buildings are built in healthy parts of the earth's body.

*\*\**

We looked in detail above at the earth's magnetic field and its effect on our health. That tends to be a form of unseen pollution in our world, i.e. it is not visible but it can ultimately lead to our ill health. Similarly, $CO_2$ emissions are hard for us to appreciate as it is an invisible gas that is pumped out into our atmosphere. This is another reason why people are finding it so hard to engage with the fight to reduce global emissions; because they cannot see this gas around them every day.

However, every day we can all see the very real and visible pollution we, as a species, are creating in the form of waste from our daily lives. Nobody has to look very far to see how much waste we generate in our lives[6]. If we again work from the individual level, we can tackle and break this problem down into manageable chunks. If one was to look at the annual waste from a western world country piled up in one place it, would lead to a very hopeless prognosis of trying to fix the problem. Alternatively, if an individual were to look at their own annual waste piled up into their back garden, they would feel much more confident in trying to tackle the problem. We are all aware of the main things we can do to reduce our waste; namely to reduce packaging, to use all the food we purchase, to recycle, and to turn our organic waste into compost. There is nothing new in any of those measures and, they have been adopted by mankind for centuries.

At the moment, though, we are not handling our waste correctly. Again, that is because we still have not come into full personal empowerment to make all those choices that we should be making. The good news is that once we stop choking our earth's arteries with waste, she will very quickly recover. The earth has amazing powers of recovery. Even in horribly devastated places like the demilitarized zone between North and South Korea, observers are amazed at how quickly the earth can start to implement its self preservation and healing techniques once man is taken out of the equation. The ceasefire introduced in the Korean War in 1953 meant the withdrawal of all human activity from this 150 mile stretch of land. What was once land that was stripped clean of trees and full of land mines, bomb damage, and military waste, is now a verdant, lush and healthy landscape that is full of wild animals.

*\*\*\**

## Summary

**Current Society view of land:**
- Earth is a place to be exploited at all costs.
- All land is there to be exploited, ideally to build upon and subsequently profit from.
- All technology and its supporting devices are deemed fit for public consumption regardless of location or as of yet unknown health reducing side effects.
- Technology advancement trumps preservation of parts of the earth as a mainstream belief pattern.
- Waste is someone else's problem. What is unseen is not on our conscience.

**Sustainable Community view of land:**
- Reverence for the earth that sustains the individual and the community. Intimacy with surroundings.
- Knowledge of earth weak points. Avoidance of these for home or work buildings.
- Technology supporting devices like boosters, transmitters etc. are necessary to enable communication etc. but should be restricted to certain designated spots only.
- Classification of earth weak points, refusal to allow human inhabitation on these places. Charting and healing or remedial work to be carried out on many of the places contaminated by man.
- We all own our waste and have to process it accordingly. The earth will purge and can handle all of our waste if we make the initial steps to reduce the excessive quantities we currently expect it to process for us.

# Sixteen: Integrating Developing Countries

One of the greatest concerns of the green movement is not the western worlds' $CO_2$ emissions levels, but the fear about the total world wide emissions levels once developing countries start to become bigger consumers of goods and services[1]. Many fear we will reach a tipping point in emissions that will push our climate into an irreversible change that will ultimately kill off our species.

This is all very alarming stuff. Should we be concerned? At this stage, you will probably get the thrust of my belief system. I believe the earth can accommodate the populations of the world of today and of the future, but cannot sustain us if we pursue our current distribution of the bounties of the world.

So, yes, we do need to take drastic action, but we need to do so with a health warning. So many of the solutions being mooted and implemented politically, albeit with noble intentions, to reduce $CO_2$ emissions are already potential failures. The carbon credit scheme is an example of this[2]. We saw in an earlier chapter how this scheme has many inherent flaws and may not ever achieve its desired goal of guaranteeing and ultimately reducing greenhouse gas emissions.

Again, this is why we need to drive forward local solutions to world wide problems. Just allowing legislation from the top down to limit our emissions of $CO_2$ is crazy. It is open to all forms of lobbying, incompetence and corruption for a start. Further, it is a very blinkered view of our problems. It seems equivalent to put blinkers on a skittish horse. While he can now concentrate on moving forward without distraction, he is limited to around 30 degrees of view. He is missing so much on his journey, and also, he could be causing damage to his surroundings that are on his visual blind spots. Similarly with concentrating solely on $CO_2$ emissions, we end up being blinkered. While we may end reducing this gas world wide, we ignore methane emissions (far more detrimental to the environment)[3] or indeed subsequent secondary pollution of water ways and land by implementing ill suited solutions for reducing $CO_2$ emissions.

The earth should be a classic example to us. We often make a change somewhere on its surface, for example putting a hydroelectric dam in place. We assume we can just make this intrusion on its surface and since it is a good thing (providing renewable electricity) we fail to see the devastating impact and trigger effect it can have on the eco systems of the area. The point is, we cannot understand the vastly superior and amazingly complex balance of nature that the earth seems able to regulate. That is why I believe we are starting to become so alarmed at our $CO_2$ emissions. We truly do realise our ignorance to the effects of our impact. It is why we *hope* that if we reduce $CO_2$, then we will get ourselves into balance. It is naïve. What we need to do is form solutions from the ground up, to manage our local community first and foremost.

If we treat where we live with integrity, and start working with nature, we will start to regain our place in the cycle of nature. We will see how the earth repairs itself, cleanses itself, and purges toxins from its environment. We will start to preserve, with better care, the bounties she yields to us; from recycling rain water, to processing our own waste before returning it to the soil, to generating our own power, growing our own food, and ultimately, to limiting our consumption of goods that are not good for the environment.

It is not good enough anymore to sit and wait for big business and government to tell us how to be good little green consumers. We need to find our own solutions and not buy in to years of ill suited bureaucratic solutions to what are ultimately local problems. We talk about $CO_2$ emissions as being some vast impossible task to tackle. However, in essence, we are talking about an excess of a gas in our atmosphere. This global atmosphere is the sum of the atmospheres from all the little housing estates, suburbs, countryside and cities in the world. Therefore, the atmosphere is not a global problem; it is a series of local problems added together. By fixing our atmosphere locally, it inspires others to do the same, and ultimately we will get to the point where we can fix the global atmosphere. If we treat the solution as only being possible at a local level, it means we will remove the blinkers of the current solutions.

We will see the other things in our environment that need to be fixed along the way too; namely water quality and pollution of the earth.

***

Should developing countries be allowed to consume goods and services like us in the western world? We were all supposed to be created equal, to all equally share in the infinite bounty of the earth and live in paradise here. That was the plan, anyway, but as we know, somewhere along the line it went askew. In the western world we have advanced at a tremendous pace to lead very high standards of living. We take for granted devices like washing machines, cars, fridges, microwaves, televisions, tumble dryers and dish washers. We feel entitled to use these devices and would fight for our right to keep using them. In the developing world, economies are only now starting to experience the manic growth phase that the west went through midway through the 20th century. They are starting to taste the freedom technology can bring to their lives and they desire and crave more solutions and gadgets. Should they have to give up all this?

After all, the West has created most of the environmental problems in the world and has already enjoyed its exponential growth phases. The poorer countries would justifiably argue that they are entitled to all the same goods and services and an equally high standard of living. Unfortunately, if one is to look at where most of the truly devastating environmental pollution in the world is, they will find that it is in these developing countries. We in the West may enjoy the spoils of technology, but generally we don't have to experience the vices of the factories, by-products and pollution that create our toys. In developing countries people often have less of a voice, regulation is often minimal (as opposed to excessive in the West) and the local governments allow companies to run their businesses there to get people working and to experience the growth they desire.

So, while they may wish for all the gadgets and freedom of technology, they are already paying a heavy price for hosting the factories that build these devices for our consumption in the West. That is the irony; they are allowing a raping and pillaging of their land to be able to sell goods to us and then in turn they can purchase these same goods from their generated wealth. Along the way a lot of devastation is happening[4]. The poor are often voiceless and they are just getting on with life despite contamination to their water, air and land from dirty factories. Of course this is not fair. Why should they be polluting their land just to be able to build their GDP or to be able to export to the West?

I believe the solution is found by looking again at ourselves locally. If we in the West continue to provide a market for polluting goods, then we are adding to the problem. If we engage more and more with our communities, we may find the desire to import these types of goods reduces dramatically. Similarly, if the people of these developing countries start to organise themselves more and more into communities with activist voices, they can possibly arrest the desecration of their lands.

The one advantage that the developing countries of the world have over us in the West is that their sense of community is largely intact. As we became more and more wealthy, we found we were able to shut our doors and not depend on outside help. We could simply purchase whatever assistance we needed. In poorer countries, people do not have the wealth and so have the sense of shared resources and of community assisting each other. They just need to find more of a forceful voice to stand up for their rights. We, here in the west need to start working together.

Perhaps here there is a meeting of minds. We need to learn from these people how to share, assist, and live in community. They need to learn from us on how to stand up for their rights and assert themselves. Together, we can hopefully force big business to stop polluting our beautiful earth. So the answer to the question is Yes, I do believe these people deserve the modern gadgets that make life easier. However, they cannot get them on the current path of providing them. It will finish us all. There has to be a middle road where the production of the worlds' goods and services is not done so carelessly and with detrimental consequences to the water, air and earth. We, the people of the world, hold the key; don't purchase those items that are polluting and also don't allow those companies work in our localities.

If we look at the totally complex and infinite amount of species the earth can sustain, then we can potentially have the faith that she can provide for all ten billion of us come 2050. As we make more and more advances in technology, these advances have to be pollution free. I, for one, totally trust that our ingenuity will yield a pollution free energy source for the world within 20 years. The future can be bright. If we stop being so passive and fix our own environment, the cumulative effect will be truly wonderful. Then maybe we all can be equal and share in the infinite bounty of the earth.

***

## Summary

**Current Society View:**
Western business viewpoint on developing countries:
- Place to source cheap labour from, and build manufacturing plants there, to sell products to the west at great profit.
- Crowded and busy parts of the earth where pollution is tolerated more and regulation is a lot more relaxed.

Developing countries:
- Desire a lot of the advancements of the west. Suffering in the process from excessive pollution.
- Not as engaged actively or powerful enough in forcing big business to change.

**Sustainable Community View:**
- A convergence in living standards between wealthier and poorer nations, but not to the detriment of the earth.
- Constantly investing in and seeking non polluting energy sources and technology advancement.
- Sharing of skill sets, e.g. community co-operatives from the developing countries and analytical business skills from the west.

# Seventeen: World-wide Development Plan

Where is society going? Does anyone think about that question for more than a few seconds every now and again?

In truth, throughout history people relied on the wisdom of a few to guide the collective. Over time, this morphed into following and listening to the hierarchy in a religion. Also, we gave our power to the governments of our world to decide where we, as a society, were going. Unfortunately, none of these institutions are best placed to perform this task. Governments generally only look at where the *economy* is heading. It is of paramount importance in our current world, to the detriment of all else. We focus on items like GDP, national debt, trade balances, housing starts, unemployment data, salary levels and spending power. The irony is we don't even end up with long term plans for all of this. More often than not, we are reacting to the position of these relative indices. If they are positive, all is well with the world and confidence is high. If they are down, nothing is right with the world and confidence is shattered. It goes back to the analogy of us living our lives in the choppy waters of the ocean's surface. We will always be reacting to events in this location and we have no power.

We need society plans and plans for our evolution. Again, we need to build these from the ground up. If we can get into true sustainable communities with our neighbours and our immediate environments, this means we have broken the dominance of the economy as the primary force in our lives. Instead of feeling like we are in a constant transition, which so many of our housing solutions make us feel like, we can start to envisage a future where the location we live right now can and will meet all our needs for the future. The way to get that sense of place is to work with our community on making a community development plan for all.

If we are in community with 150 or so people, a development plan may incorporate some of the following:

- Appraisal of skills and services of community members
- Definition of rules and regulations of a bartering system that would get implemented based on the information garnered from point 1 above

- Holistic education plan for children
- Goal setting around percentages of local food production, water recycling, energy generation and waste recycling
- Scheduling of community group time for recreation, barbecues etc.
- Plans for sustainable transport solutions for community
- Plan to integrate ageing population
- Plan for building of shared community building(s)
- Development plan for usage of shared community building(s)
- Support mechanism for care of pre-school children

These development plans would be in place for five, or perhaps ten years. It can be seen from above that far from just looking at the economic plans for the people, it covers a whole range of other important areas of life. Obviously, these plans will evolve over time and will have different goals and ambitions depending on the demographics of the people in community. Each community would have their own development plans and it would make sense that there would be a huge similarity of plans in communities' worldwide. The needs of people are very similar country to country.

If we have experience of having long term communal planning, it makes sense that we would expect our nationalities as a whole, and indeed our world itself, to have a society goal. If you were to ask anyone today what the world's goal should be, I think you would stump 99.9% of people. Nobody asks such a question. That is all the more reason for us to tease out that very question.

**Perhaps for the next twenty years or so our goal should be to secure a non polluting energy source and to also really clean up our environment.**

We have many disparate groups world wide trying to find THE magical breakthrough to finding a truly sustainable energy generating source. While that is commendable, in a lot of cases it is being done for purely commercial reasons only. Perhaps we need a much more co-ordinated worldwide long term action plan. Rest assured, the one company or institution that cracks this mystery, could well end up becoming the richest and most powerful corporation in the world of the future. Now is the time for us all to try and stake a claim in the collective race to find this solution to our energy needs. Remember, in an earlier chapter we spoke about philanthropy feeding money back into society from the back end. It was after the money had been made from society. Similarly, why should one company be allowed to use the natural resources of the world to generate energy (sustainably) for the world of the future and earn vast profits from it?

Surely, collective society would be much better served if we all owned and shared in these new power sources. It would keep energy cheap permanently for the future. It would have the knock on effect of reducing one of businesses' and householders' largest costs and, therefore, require us all to earn far less money in the future to pay for the commodity. Remember, any energy source that is sustainable is free, e.g. it will come inevitably from the sun, wind or the water (or some other unforeseen natural sustainable resource), so why should we all have to pay for it exponentially well into the future once we have paid off the technology that is generating it?

One need only look at oil for an example. Oil is a gift from the earth. While it is not renewable as a source, it was one of the bounties she yielded for us. It was commercialised initially in the US[1] and was quickly adopted for its energy giving qualities. Vast fortunes have been and are currently made from its sale to wider society by a few companies that have evolved from those initial prospectors. Oil prices have the ability to cripple economies, or to allow them experience huge growth. It is a cornerstone of the world's economy. If we all owned this bounty of the earth, it would not have forced so many people to work so hard for so long. We should not make the same mistake with the next cycle of the world's energy. It has the ability to be a strong tool in our fight to free us from the inflation driven world of today. Hence, if our local communities can become more vociferous and engage more with our national governments, then hopefully we can work together long term at an international level to get collective ownership as a species over the world's resources and their distribution. Therefore, collectively tackling this great modern conundrum facing society

— securing the energy needs of the future — is a very noble world wide plan for everyone to work towards solving and ultimately to benefit from equally.

Similarly, by cleaning up our environment worldwide, it would also set in motion positive changes to do with access to good water and, ultimately, this would start to help alleviate world hunger. That is just my opinion on two areas that we should work on together around the world as part of our generic society long term goals for the next twenty years or so.

*\*\**

Let's revisit the governance model I proposed in an earlier chapter where the people matured into their power and ran their local communities, while the elected governments yielded power and stepped down to meet the people. I proposed that the future national governments be comprised of people who had experience of governing local communities. The same is true for long term planning. These same people who have experience and success at local long term effective planning should be charged with running our national executives to forge long term national and international plans.

It will be a position of great responsibility in the future; that of filtering the desires and information from the bottom up, i.e. from the sustainable communities of the world and transferring that information into long term national and world plans.

Then, at the end of a long term plan, we would collectively develop one for the next 20 years or so. Perhaps during the years 2030-2050, after we have worked on energy and pollution, we could look at a final weaning away from population growth dependency and more to integration of ageing populations as people live longer and longer while birth rates fall. Of course, all the while that we work on these goals collectively as a species, we are still living through and implementing our own individual community plans.

Currently, we have countries that implement plans in isolation for the future or indeed like the Kyoto Protocol we do get collective plans to reduce carbon dioxide emissions worldwide over a certain long term period. The problem with these plans is they have not engaged with the people who ultimately need to change their ways. We are being directed from the top down on how to fix something without allowing us to provide the solutions ourselves in our daily lives. People are legislated into submission. This only leads to rebellion and a dispassionate participation by people at best, or an outright refusal to comply often being the case.

*** 

## Summary

**Current Society Long Term Development:**
- Happens organically with no real vision for individual or collective future.
- Economic planning takes precedence over everything else (and even this is not long term planning).
- World's resources there for the taking by the most resourceful, powerful or cunning.

**Sustainable Community Long Term Development:**
- Starts out with short term, then medium term and subsequently long term community planning.
- Long term national plans merge into collective worldwide plans that have evolved from the wishes of the people.
- Sharing of earth's bounty to help attain a long term sustainable future for the species of man.

# PART TWO

# Transforming a Suburban Housing Development into a Sustainable Community

A home is often the biggest purchase in most people's lifetimes. Usually, it is a rectangular block or timber construction set in one of three typical locations; be it city, countryside or suburb. For something that is usually an average of four times ones annual salary, up to ten times in recent property booms in some countries, people often pay very little regard to their choice.

Suburbia is the newest and most recent addition to our housing stock. Because of its relative newness as a solution for housing the people of the world, it has become a microcosm of the problems faced by people. Also, suburbia would probably be the last place sustainable community would work. That is because, by its nature, it tends to make access to resources difficult and is spread out and often very poorly planned. These are all the reasons why suburbia is a challenge to achieve sustainability, but also why it must be tackled and act as a blueprint for wider integration of sustainable community development. If we can make the suburbs sustainable living models, then the cities and countryside will be far easier.

First let's look at the evolution of suburbia as a viable housing option for millions of people worldwide. Worldwide, suburbia has become very common in the pasty fifty years. Prior to World War II, people tended to be either rurally based or very definite city dwellers. As education levels became more and more elevated, they broke out of the confines of either the rural/city based manual labourer role. The rural person often moved to the city of nearest proximity, but wanted to be able to access his or her workplace while still feeling the proximity of the open area and ground. City centres were filled already. Hence the desire was born for a location bordering and with easy access to a metropolis, but within touching distance of "rural" life. Suburbia was created and became part of all spatial planners' toolkits.

It took many years for the city dwellers to cotton on to the idea of leaving their ready access to all amenities and venture the "vast" distance of up to ten miles out to the "boonies". In time, though, this became commonplace as access to affordable and available land in city centres made access to similarly affordable homes out of reach for a lot of people.

In the past couple of decades, suburbia experienced another evolution. In that time, the suburban belt around cities loosened considerably and now we have a situation where people are often commuting to cities from up to sixty miles away, often taking ninety minutes or more each way to access their workplace.

I believe many people feel cut off, isolated and trapped in this existence. In Ireland, for example, the commuter belt for Dublin city extends to the distances outlined above and this situation is also very common in a lot of American and European cities.

\*\*\*

Hill Valley Plains, BallyNotter.
Distance to Dublin:  39 miles
Built: 2003
Housing units: 49
Population 2009: 145

This is a *fictional* tale of a housing development built in Ireland in 2003 as a feeder location for people commuting to, and working in Dublin. It is a largely rural area, but falls into the definition of a suburb of the city by the lifestyle choices of its inhabitants, e.g. commuting daily to the city for work. A common thread of these new suburbs in Ireland, and indeed worldwide, is the appalling lack of planning involved in designing them as communities where people can have a high quality of life. What has been of more importance has been the building of housing units as an end in itself and their subsequent sale for very high profits. Very often, access to proper sustainable services is the last consideration. While this tale is fictional, it could be one of any housing development in any city or country in the western world.

***

The place was timeless. Fifty acres or so of the most verdant and lush land imaginable which was settled and nuzzled into the bend of a tributary river flowing towards the Shannon, Ireland's main river. The small river doubled back on itself several times in this location and from the air resembled a snake in motion. The old Gaelic name given to the locality was *Baile an nathair*, roughly translated as the town land of the snake. The people of old did this in Ireland and worldwide; locations were named for the physical formations found there. When Ireland was part of the UK, a policy of renaming town lands away from the Gaelic format was rolled out. This was to ascribe English names to the areas. However, instead of using English words to physically describe the town lands, the officials just anglicised the sound of the existing terms. Hence Baile an nathair became BallyNotter; a truly meaningless term.

The land was prone to very occasional flooding; perhaps only once every twenty years or so, but certainly enough to be known amongst the local farmers who lived in the area. It was a flat part of the country, part of the great expansive central plain of Ireland. Settlements had come and gone over the millennia, initially they were of very low impact due to the dense covering of native oak on the land. The authorities laid waste to large swathes of the native forest of Ireland during the 16-18<sup>th</sup> centuries and the timber was exported abroad, mainly for the purpose of wine casket construction and shipbuilding.

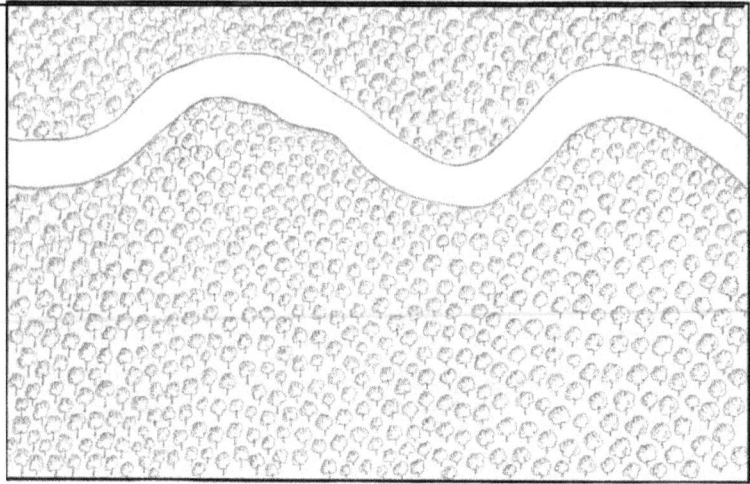

The land at BallyNotter circa 1500.

As a result, this small pocket of land was made more accessible and was incorporated into farm holdings and passed through the generations. A small village sprung up in the early decades of the 1900's that was also known as BallyNotter and was situated nearly a mile from the fifty acre plot. It had a church, a primary school, a pub and a small shop. A road from BallyNotter joined a main motorway to Dublin about five miles away and from there, it was around thirty-four miles to the city.

The last man to farm the fields was John Murphy who was born in 1922. He was a bachelor. He lived a simple life and enjoyed a couple of drinks in the pub every other night. John eked out a living on his land and made do with whatever came his way. He relied on the friendship of people in his locality and was always certain to be seen whenever a social gathering was happening.

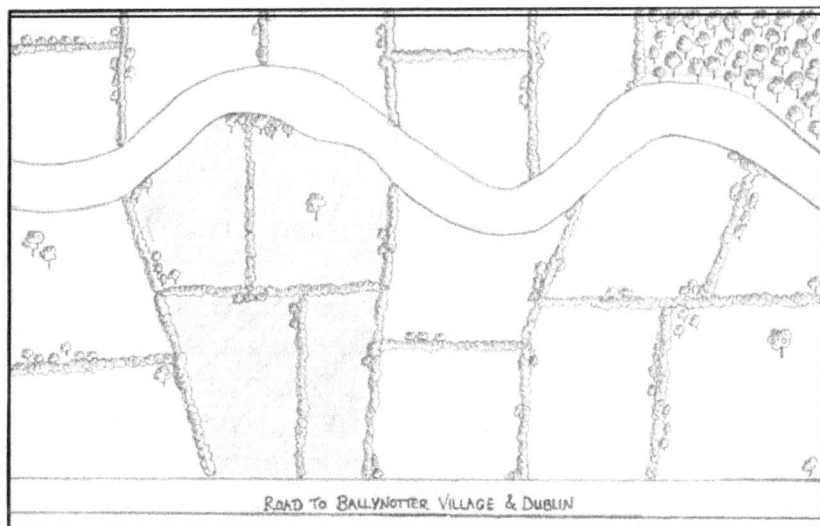

ROAD TO BALLYNOTTER VILLAGE & DUBLIN

Change of land from tree cover to farmland. Fields shaded as farmed by John Murphy circa 1960.

He died in December1999 after a sudden sharp winter flu that morphed into pneumonia. His funeral was well attended as he was highly regarded in the area. John had only one sibling, a sister named Mary, who had moved to Dublin over fifty years earlier when he was twenty-one, she eighteen. She had gotten a job in the civil service. This was very exciting for her and opened whole new vistas, far greater than any life she could have imagined in BallyNotter. She moved into RathCross, a suburb of Dublin (six miles from the city centre) that was on the road home to BallyNotter. Mary married a country lad from county Cork, a teacher, and they ended up having only one child, a son named Brian. He was a solicitor and by the time of John's passing he was forty-eight and married with two children.

Brian had no interest in either of his parent's origins. He was a man of the times, moving in fast circles and very busy with his work practice and social life. He never really saw much of John as an adult, even though he had spent a lot of time on the farm as a kid where they holidayed every summer during harvest time.

John only knew one way, and that was the family way. All through the years he supported his sister's move to the city from afar and was proud of her achievements and those of his only credible heir, Brian. Knowing John, the only way his will would be read out was to leave his holding of forty-seven acres to Brian, his nephew. And so it transpired that several months after the cold day in BallyNotter where they had laid John to rest, Brian accompanied by his mother, visited the offices of Michael Murphy, a local solicitor in the nearby town of Glenmore, to hear the contents of his Uncle's will.

Within months the land was on the open market. Brian had already spent the two years prior to John's death lobbying and bribing local councillors in the county area of BallyNotter to rezone John Murphy's farm from agricultural to low density residential land. This had the desired effect of making the land about five times more valuable. Since most of these councillors knew John well, Brian also paid them off so they would not tell him anything about the plan.

He knew he was promised the land and knew John would not be around forever, hence his desire to move ahead of the game and have the land rezoned. Even though the land was prone to the odd flood, the motion to rezone it passed by a vote of nine to six at the council meeting. It had cost Brian 100,000 Euros in bribes and he didn't manage to get all forty-seven acres rezoned, but to get twenty-six acres with the rest remaining as green space was still an excellent result.

A property developer acquired all forty-seven acres for 5.2 million Euro. Brian used this as a springboard and launched into complex property syndicate investment portfolios abroad. His social standing rose, too and he moved in more rarefied financial circles. He never again gave a thought for his uncle John. This is where we leave the life of Brian.

***

Kevin Maguire purchased the land. He was from a small village about five miles from BallyNotter. He was a grafter. He had made his way to Chicago in the early 1980's from the poor and depressed Ireland of the time. Having no trade when he left at nineteen, initially, the only work he could get was as a manual labourer on the building sites. Since he was an illegal immigrant, he could only work in the black market for cash. His boss was a tough cookie who took no prisoners. However, he liked the hefty lump of a lad from Ireland on sight. There was an eagerness and an edge to him that he recognised from when he himself was that age. It was confirmed later that first day when he saw the amount of work Kevin got through.

Life moved quickly in the states. If you were good you progressed, it was as simple as that. Kevin was good and kept his head down and worked long hours. Within a few years, he managed to avail of an amnesty and received his residency visa. Once the paperwork was in place, he went out on his own as an independent building contractor. He started refurbishing derelict buildings in the poorer districts, since no one else seemed willing to do the really dirty work. He stuck at it for a few years and made his way up to building housing units in the expanding middle class suburbs of Chicago.

Over time, he missed home and started thinking about returning. It was now the early 1990's, but still the word from Ireland was that things were not so great economically. He kept going for a few more years; it was easy to let the years pass quickly in the states. Life was good, money was good, and he and his new wife, Helen, who was from Limerick, a nurse he met on an Irish expat night out, were enjoying the spoils of success.

By 1997 they had one child and Helen was pregnant with their second. She wanted to go home to be close to her siblings. Kevin always figured that he would return home at some stage, and the timing seemed right. Apparently, things were really picking up in Ireland; there was lots of activity in the building sector. He had built up a sizeable nest egg from his years of hard work. He set himself up as the only thing he knew once they returned to his village; as a developer of housing units.

In the first year after returning, Kevin built a few single unit houses just to find his feet. They went well and he learned the local market fairly well. By mid 2000, when the forty-seven acres at BallyNotter came on the market, he had the financial resources and was perfectly poised to outbid anyone else for the land. There weren't too many competitors at the auction and he finalised on the deal at 5.2 million Euro. He had done his figures and reckoned on at least two million profit from developing forty-nine relatively large houses.

The housing estate was named on a whim. Hill Valley Plains sounded like a truly modern development and seemed the type of name to fit in with the zeitgeist. The irony of having a name with three different and contrasting land formations was lost on Kevin. He was a decent enough guy, but sensitively naming a location would not have been one of his areas of expertise. The only part of the name that somehow described his development was "plains", as the land was flat and open.

The design of the site was handed over to a busy architectural practice in Dublin. "Bog standard", had been the reply from Kevin when asked his vision of the development. He had no vision for the area; he just wanted to see forty-nine houses in place as soon as was practical.

The planning process was fairly easy. Once land had been rezoned, it was usually a matter of fine tuning the building appearances, etc., and within twelve months Kevin had full permission to progress. He completed the housing estate in early 2003. They were sold in three different types; three, four and five bedroom-two storey houses. Ireland was in a major boom time by then and Kevin's projected profits were rising daily as the houses hit the market. The asking prices rose significantly as the latter houses neared completion, all in the space of a few months. Some people were paying differences of 30-50K for the same houses. Kevin felt guilty charging these massive prices as he knew this was crazy boom territory, but the market accepted it and all developers nationwide were at the same practice. There seemed to be immense confidence out there, not just in Ireland, but worldwide.

It seemed such a long way from the shy nineteen year old who had to borrow the air fare to Chicago from his father over twenty years earlier.

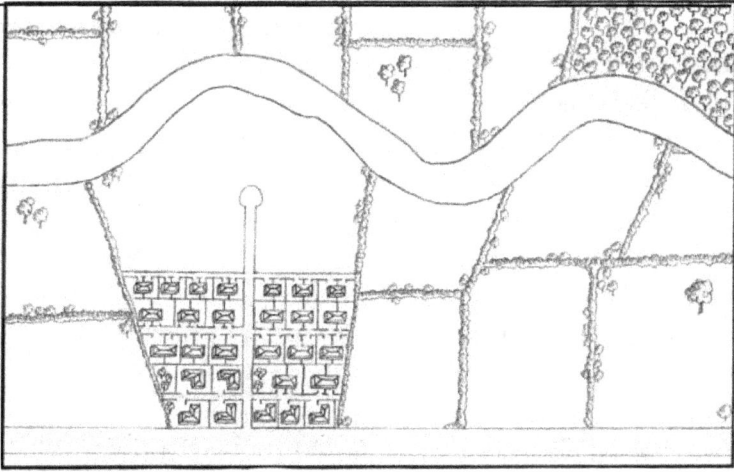

Hill Valley Plains circa 2003 just after construction

People from all walks of life, locations and backgrounds ended up either purchasing the houses or renting them from investors who had purchased them. The relative proximity to a big city and the lovely natural greenness and openness of the area was a big attraction. While the development looked like so many others across the country, and indeed like any housing estate anywhere in the western world, people still queued up to live there. There was a mix of different demographics in the houses. *A full description of all forty-nine householders as of 2009 can be seen in Appendix A.*

The one constant for all the people in Hill Valley was that the adults were either too busy with their lives if they were working, or had too much free time on their hands if they were either retired or unemployed. The kids were kids. They just loved to play, but life seemed to be run on a clock for them. Everything was part of a structured day; be it crèche or school time, commuting with their parents, or attending after school activities.

The place was possessed of a strange eeriness from Monday – Friday during daylight hours. Anyone who was based at home didn't tend to congregate outside. In fact, just a few children who were preschoolers and whose mothers or fathers were around to look after them populated the quiet streets of their housing estate.

On the weekends, things didn't really get busy either. It was common for a lot of children to be ferried off to organised activities like horse riding, swimming lessons, or sports groups in the mornings. Then around 1p.m., an exodus of cars usually started leaving the estate to head off for a family day trip somewhere, often driving the same route they had all week for work to one of the large malls on the outskirts of Dublin city.

There seemed to be an itchiness to be gone from Hill Valley Plains. People either worked or were off on leisure activities. The place only seemed to be used for watching TV at night and sleeping. Of course some people did engage with their neighbours. Irish people tend to be informal, chatty and genuinely interested in other people. The bond of friendship between the adults, though, was usually only created if there was contact in the first place between their children. Even then, it tended to be quite formal and rarely progressed to any level of intimacy.

No one really seemed to have the time or the inclination to get too close to other people. A fierce independence had crept in with people in the last generation or so. They tended to survive life's joys, trials and tribulations without leaning too much on anyone else. It was almost like admitting weakness if life couldn't be handled with only the assistance of the personnel within the confines of the four walls of home.

Several years passed and people got more and more settled. The boom was big news. It was all they talked about. Anybody who had the will worked. There was no shortage of it. Wages were high, expectations had skyrocketed, and people spent freely. The mood seemed to be shared around the world. Hill Valley Plains just morphed into peoples lives that lived there. Most drove in and out of the estate and were oblivious to their surroundings. They couldn't tell you if there were trees planted in the green spaces, and if they couldn't see the river that resembled a coiled snake from their houses, they most likely forgot it was even there.

Life seemed to be a solitary experiment lived out in a series of boxes with a few close family members. The boxes in question were the house, the car, the office, or factory and the shopping malls. If they cared to admit it to themselves, they felt disconnected. Not unhappy generally, just a sense that this life was passing them by somehow. It all seemed a little repetitive. Life seemed to resolve around a cycle of lounging on couches at night flicking through satellite TV channels, drinking a little too much occasionally, early starts, rushing to crèches and work, long working hours, bad diets, rushed family time in the evenings and then back into another day again.

The year 2008 started to bring bad tidings. By 2009, a full blown national and international crisis was brewing. Confidence had been shattered, unemployment was rife, unnecessary spending stopped, businesses closed, banks collapsed and governments teetered on the precipice repeatedly. Everybody seemed stumped and afraid.

The world was in a vacuum. Nobody knew where it would all lead. A new president in the United States peppered his speeches with kernels of wisdom that those who were ready to listen latched on to. He spoke of people needing to step up to the mark, needing to take charge of *their* own lives, of not expecting governments or institutions to fix everything for them. I say only some were able to take the message on board because the majority were still waiting for someone else to fix their lives. Most of the residents of Hill Valley Plains fell into the latter category at that time.

Three different events happened in Hill Valley Plains during the summer of 2009 that triggered key changes and improvements in the lives of some of the residents of the estate, and these changes triggered yet more happenings. Before long, a revolution was in full swing in a little hamlet thirty-nine miles from Dublin.

*\*\*\**

A subset of Appendix A is shown below with information on several of the householders.

**House #2:** A five bed occupied by Joe Kennedy, age 52, self employed as a solicitor; Mary Kennedy, age 51, self employed as a solicitor; Kevin Kennedy, age 18,

**House #7:** A five bed occupied by Michael Cox, age 35, employed as an engineer; Avril Cox, age 36, employed as a planner; their children, James 3 and Melissa 18months.

**House #11:** A four bed occupied by Pat O'Brien, age 46, self employed as a plumber; Sheila O'Brien, age 44, home maker; their children, Ciara 14, Maeve 12 and Brian 8.

**House #13:** A three bed occupied by Sean Crosby, age 65, retired school teacher.

**House #34:** A three bed occupied by Fiona Smith, age 49, employed as a nurse; her children, Leo 17 and Alison 14.

**House #36:** A four bed occupied by Ken Griffin, age 40, self employed as an accountant; Jane Brady, age 37, employed in public relations.

**House #48:** A three bed occupied by Lisa Kiernan, widow, age 61, trained as a child psychologist; her children, two adult daughters, live abroad.

***

Sean Crosby had purchased number thirteen from the plans. He felt a connection with the number in some way. Of course, many were put off by the supposed ill luck that attends that number, but Sean felt life had already dealt him his fair share of bad luck. He had taken early retirement at fifty-nine. He had loved the vocation of teaching, but found it had become too soulless. In latter years he saw himself as a technician like figure; charged to program impressionable minds for state examinations.

The opportunities to find the joy he felt in his younger days when he broke through to a troubled youth, or quietly praised the shyest kids were all but gone. It had become an industry, a production line, so to speak, and there was no place anymore for a romantic who wanted to inspire children.

His career had been in Cork, a city nearly two hours from BallyNotter. He had sold up his townhouse in the city and returned to BallyNotter to live out his retirement. Sean had grown up on a farm a few miles from Hill Valley Plains and always wanted to return at some point. He was able to purchase his new home for cash and had a little left over from his own home sale. This extra nest egg supplemented his pension nicely and he was well set up financially for his latter years.

Life in BallyNotter was not how he had expected it to be. A lot of the people he had known no longer lived locally, had died, or were busy with their own lives. He quickly found that his loneliness had followed him up from Cork.

Sean had never gotten over her. Ann was a beautiful girl from Kerry. She lit up his life. They were only going out with each other for three years when she was killed in a car accident one morning on her way to the school they both taught in. They were engaged to be married and felt they had the world at their feet. They both loved children, something that had drawn them to their careers, and they were planning to start a family as soon as they could.

Ann died when Sean was twenty-seven. They say time heals all wounds, and while it is true to some extent, he just never had the heart to go into a serious relationship again. There were plenty of women who tried over the years, but somehow he always managed to make himself unavailable, at which point they simply lost interest.

His morning routine nowadays was to go and buy the paper in the village and follow that with a brisk five mile walk, whatever the weather. He made his lunch on his return and dinner whenever he could be bothered. Television had never interested him, and instead, he tended to read books voraciously in the evenings. And that was pretty much it. A cycle of solitude that was broken only by occasional Sunday visits either to, or from his siblings.

\*\*\*

Fiona Smith was forty-nine. She lived with her two children, Leo, who was seventeen, and Alison who was fourteen. They had purchased number thirty-four two years earlier when they had moved over from the UK. Fiona wanted a fresh start for them all, and she had secured a job working as a staff nurse in a hospital on the outskirts of the city. She had searched the hinterland around Dublin during a two week holiday for a suitable place to live and settled on BallyNotter. Number thirty-four was for sale and she liked the look of the area, its quietness, and its relative proximity to Dublin.

It certainly seemed a lot nicer than the very busy suburban area they left in Manchester, which seemed to extend forever. There were a lot of social problems in that area and Fiona had hoped to give her two children a less pressurised environment to grow up in. She had no ties whatsoever to Ireland, and literally, applied for a job over the internet one night at work in Manchester. She had received an offer of employment within three weeks. It was April 2007 and she had to take up the role no later than July 15th that summer. It was hard breaking the news to Leo and Alison. Her daughter wailed, screamed and protested wildly about having to leave her friends and school. Leo just sat there and didn't really seem to register an emotion either way. He had been like this for a year or so at that stage; appearing to be totally lost. Fiona hoped a new start would do him good; in fact, she hoped that it would do them all some good.

Tom had left her when Leo was five and Alison only two. They just didn't get each other anymore. It was horrible after that for several years, but she had two little kids to keep strong for and she managed to pull through. Leo had adored his dad and they had played football a lot with each other, walking over to the local park in the evenings once Tom came home from work. He really was heartbroken when his dad didn't live at home anymore. While he saw him on the weekends, he always wondered why he couldn't just come home again with him afterwards. Alison, being only two when he left, had adapted very quickly to life with just one parent.

Fiona and Alison settled right into life in Ireland. They shared a common ability to make friends easily and before long, Fiona had a nice network of friends from the hospital that she socialised with and Alison made a few friends from the estate. She loved her new school, too, and within a few months, never gave a thought for Manchester and her lost life there.

Leo just resumed his detachment and sullenness with renewed vigour in Ireland. At least in Manchester, there was more to occupy him and Fiona didn't notice it as much, but as he wandered around like a lost puppy in BallyNotter, his wounds seemed almost palpable. Unfortunately, she just didn't know how to relate to him anymore, nor him to her. After Tom left, Leo and her had been very close for years. Thankfully, he never blamed her for his dad not being part of their lives. After Tom re-married and moved to London when Leo was ten, he ended up becoming even more dependent on her. He always told her his little troubles and she was his rock in the world. However, since he reached fourteen or so, he had just clammed up.

Fiona assumed initially that it was just teenage angst and moodiness. Over time, she began to realise it was a little more serious than that. However, she lived in hope that it would all pass once he reached eighteen or nineteen. He was now seventeen and was just completing his secondary education. She felt once he got a steady girlfriend, or went away to college, things would change. Physically he had ended up becoming more and more like his dad; tall and quite handsome with wavy brown hair. She knew he had a heart of gold and had a great sense of humour, but it all seemed lost under a permanent grey cloud hanging over him.

Leo himself just didn't know where he was going or what his life would bring. His dad leaving him had left him shattered and he had lost a male role model forever. Seeing him on weekends just did not cut it. He knew somewhere that he loved his mum and sister, but couldn't feel that anymore. They always seemed so happy and he couldn't understand why. Life was crap to him. It just seemed to be a never ending cycle of boring and meaningless events.

*** 

The first spark of change in BallyNotter was the day Sean spoke to Leo. He had noticed this lad many mornings on his walk as he went for his paper. He obviously wasn't working, but then again, maybe he had just finished his schooling and was waiting for college. Sean recognised the despondent look of the boy from his teaching days and how his body language hinted at a morose outlook on life. He had also seen him come and go with his mother and sister in the car and he seemed to occupy his own grey world in the back of the car, where he always sat on his own.

Sean saw him coming from about a hundred yards away. He had time to both block the boy's path and figure out what to say. He asked him outright for assistance. No messing about, just a request for help to clear up some building debris from around his house.

Leo was startled but agreed with a nod. Nobody ever spoke to him in this area and here was a little old guy asking him for help. He wasn't sure if he would be up to the task, but he felt he should try to help him out at least.

That first day Leo didn't say much as he tidied up the garden in number thirteen, but Sean had already decided he wanted to keep him close. He felt he was needed. He asked him if he would be willing to cut his grass once a week over the summer as he was unable to because he had strained his back recently. Leo was a little reluctant, but when he weighed up the old man he decided he was genuine in his request. He agreed to a weekly rate of ten euro to cut the grass.

That summer of 2009 changed both their lives forever. Through June they rarely spoke, Sean just opening the shed to allow Leo access to the lawnmower and bringing him petrol to refill it on occasion. July became really hot. One day when Leo was finishing up, Sean decided to bring him out a cold drink and a snack. They ended up chatting in the back garden for an hour. It started out about the job just finished, but then an ease settled in between them and pretty soon they were discussing sport, school and careers. Leo told Sean he was expecting his results from leaving his secondary education, but that he had no hope of attaining any marks sufficient to allow him progress to college. While he knew he was smart enough, he admitted to doing no study during the previous year. He had spent all his evenings in his room playing computer games, while pretending to his mother that he was studying.

Sean quickly realised Leo was missing a confidant outside of his home. He became that conduit for him. He allowed the boy to say what he liked without judging him. He queried him gently on where he thought his strengths lay in life, but never pressured him in any way. Leo was right. He did fail his exams, much to the horror of Fiona who despaired, but Sean didn't berate him or judge him. In fact, when Leo mentioned it around the middle of August, Sean just nodded and assured him his path would reveal itself if he wanted it badly enough. Leo thought about this later that night and realised he wasn't ready just yet, he felt he needed time to find himself and he also wanted to spend more time in Sean's company, since he was able to speak more freely with him than anyone else.

Of course Fiona became alarmed when she had heard about the meetings between her son and the single elderly man who lived down the road. Society had taught her to be wary of people and of their intentions, but pretty soon she came around to the idea of their spending time together when she noticed a subtle, but definite improvement in Leo's mood. He still had no time for her, but at least now he seemed a little less despondent.

Sean decided he was getting just as much from his time with Leo as he felt he was giving to the boy. He had noticed his life seemed a little less repetitive when they had their weekly chats and it really seemed to break up his monotonous routines. Leo definitely had a spark about him that came to the surface more and more. His sense of humour was intact and he enjoyed teasing Sean whenever he got the chance. He had also decided that he wasn't going back to school in the autumn to repeat his exams. Whenever he thought about it his stomach knotted up and he knew a life of study or office/factory work was not for him.

Sean was great about it and didn't try to change his mind. Fiona did try to change his mind, though, and spent several days at it, but all to no avail. She felt he would drift from menial job to menial job with no direction. However, he had started to have faith in himself and felt he would find his niche in time.

Sean suggested in early September that since they both had so much free time now, they could spend a bit more time together and do a little work around the housing estate. He had lied about his back being sore back in June to get Leo to help him out and he told another white lie now to say it was strong enough again to work. He had felt that since the boy had no imminent plans and didn't know where he was going, at least he could now say he was performing some job or task if asked by anyone. It would surely give him a little more self esteem than doing nothing.

The estate was full of green spaces, but whatever planting there was in place was sporadic at best, and there was a lot of maintenance required everywhere. Weeds and a general untidiness had settled in. Since money was no impediment to Sean, he decided to pay Leo a token salary for his help. He paid him 100 euro a week and they worked a few hours a day together.

***

Avril cried every day that first week she returned to work after her maternity leave. Of course she snuck off to the bathroom to do it so no one could see her. It helped that she was expressing milk for Melissa; she could spend half an hour in there without arousing suspicion among the girls in the office. It had been the same when she had to go back to the office after having James. Maternity leave was great, eight months off, but it was an absolute nightmare to go back to full time employment in one fell swoop. One Monday morning she was living her life at the pace of baby Melissa and the following Monday morning she was back at her desk facing a forty hour week in the logistics department. This was coupled with twelve hours commuting weekly, while poor Melissa was experiencing the big bad world for the first time in a crèche.

After a week or two, both she and Melissa fell into their new routines. Michael, her husband, had only gotten three days paternity leave form his office and so he never had that wrench from family life back to working life that she had experienced.

There was little doubt that she needed to return to work. They had purchased number seven in Hill Valley Plains when the estate

116

was first built. It was the summer of 2003 and they had just gotten married. They had rolled their wedding, honeymoon and loan for the house all into one mortgage package. They were both thirty, professional and childless and they felt the world was theirs for the taking. They also purchased the biggest type of home in the development, a five bed roomed detached house with a garage. It wasn't like they planned on having four children to fill the other rooms, in fact they were finished now they had two; it just seemed to be the thing that was expected, to buy as large a house as one could afford.

Hindsight is a great thing. Avril often regretted staying in five star hotels on their honeymoon and putting those bills on their mortgage. She often regretted buying their large house, especially when she returned home from a long day in the office and realised that even though two bedrooms were not getting used, they still needed to be dusted. She regretted all of this because it was keeping her trapped in a working lifestyle that she despised. She hated the regimented schedule; 8:30 a.m. – 4:30 p.m., followed by a frantic dash to pick up James and Melissa by 5:30 p.m. from the crèche. Two hours of family time followed, well not exactly full family time as Michael often didn't get home from his job until 7 p.m. He would put the kids to bed and she would open a bottle of wine for them. This was meant to help them de-stress, to find some semblance of a life lived "off the clock", before the roller coaster started again the following morning.

Michael was a nice guy. He was bright, capable and a great dad. However, he never thought too much about their future. He liked his job as a software developer and made good money doing it. He didn't mind their lifestyle too much, it never dawned on him that he was missing out on family life. Like a lot of men, he took on the expectation from an early age that he would provide for his family as best he could and just get on with working life.

Avril was always a deep thinker. She was bright, sassy and very caring. She wanted to work, just not the hours she was expected to put in, and loved the companionship of the office and the relationships she forged there. This was especially true now that a lot of her female colleagues also had kids of their own. She found over time that the conversations at lunch had moved on from social nights out, to discussions about the best food to give a two year old, or the best type of sunscreen a baby should wear. She loved it that they were all maturing together. The irony was they were all working together, but never once spoke about work on their break times; it was always about their family life and kids.

The second event that changed life in BallyNotter during the summer of 2009 was the day Avril went to work with a big hangover. It was a Monday morning in early August, and she and Michael had been at a wedding on the Saturday that rolled into the early hours of the Sunday. By Monday morning, the full horrible effects of her weekend of excess hit like a ton of bricks. Baby Melissa and James seemed particularly cranky, too, as she dropped them off at the crèche. She drove to Dublin from the crèche, which was about half way to the city, crying in frustration all the way. She felt life had to be better in some way than this.

She spent that day looking at websites to see if there was another job she could find. Pretty quickly it became apparent that all potential employers expected a full time commitment and many offices were an even further commute from home than where she was. Despairing, she gave up, but suddenly had a brain wave. What if she could do her job in less time? She spent the next week researching this idea and listing all the tasks she performed every week. She broke this list down further into tasks she could perform remotely and tasks that had to be done in the office. Amazingly, 70% of her weekly tasks could be done from a remote location. That meant she only needed to be in the office three out of every ten working days!

Avril treated this analysis of her career like a research project. She kept it from Michael because she didn't want to discuss it with anyone until she had put her proposal to her bosses. She wanted to get this done on her own; it was almost like if she spoke about it, it would put her off. She typed up ten pages describing her role, defining her salary and then outlining the various facets of it she could do sitting at home in BallyNotter and those to be done in the office. She put a proposal together on page seven of the document. Here are some key points from her proposal.

"To work two days a week in the office in Dublin…to work remotely from home to complete the other 70% of my tasks…to stop being a full time employee…hence saving company money on pension payments, health insurance, etc,.…to work as an independent contractor at 10% less money that I currently receive.…"

Pages nine and ten was her confessional. Here she wrote her story. It explained her desire to work, the joy she got from her colleagues, how she liked her job, but despised the clock driven formality of a forty hour week. It further outlined how she adored her little kids and wanted so badly to spend more time with them, how she was a night owl and could spend 3-4 hours working at night from 10 or 11 p.m. onwards, get her job finished, but still be there in the morning and afternoon for James and Melissa.

She cried writing it, but for the first time they were not tears of desperation, but more so tears coming from a position of strength. Even if they did not accept her proposal, it felt damn good to find a solution herself to her own problems. She couldn't go back now; if they refused her, then she would find another company or another way.

After many edits, she printed off the letter, sealed it in an envelope and marched right past the three layers of middle managers over her and straight to the cubicle of the managing director. She knew her request would get lost in translation if passed up through the chain of command. After handing her MD the envelope, she asked him if he would please do her the favour of truly evaluating her proposal. A week later he scheduled an appointment with her in the canteen and amazingly acquiesced with a large smile on his face.

He said he personally felt a revolution was on the way in offices worldwide. What she was proposing would be the norm within ten years. Everything she wrote about was stuff he juggled and struggled with himself, unfortunately for him, his seniority tied him to his desk. He shook her hand and said she had all his support to be a test case for this working model for him. He had spoken with his superiors in headquarters in the United States and they, too, supported this move in theory. They knew many people were on the brink of despair from the defined career schedules and they didn't want to start losing quality staff.

Avril glided home that evening in the car in a never ending sequence of tears of joy, squeals, smiles and shouting out loud every few minutes. She didn't tell Michael until later that night. He was delighted for her, but didn't see what was so unique about her situation. Many people had worked part time or even job shared. Avril then explained that this was a whole new shift in work practices, she was not part time or job sharing. She was still working full time, but all on her terms. Being bright and very capable meant she could complete her role in about twenty-five hours a week without the many social distractions of the office. She only needed to go to Dublin two days a week and so had five other days in the week to work those extra nine or ten hours. That worked out at an average of two hours work a day at home over five days. All of this for only a 10% pay cut! *Her pay cut had been her idea to make the move more attractive to the company; however, they would have given her the new structure without this cut.* Also, since she was now a sole trader, she could research and pick a good pension policy and manage her own tax affairs.

As she went to bed that night she realised she had moved from the role of a passive victim of circumstances, into the role of someone who was powerfully directing their life.

\*\*\*

Pat recognised her from the estate. She lived there with her husband, although he wasn't too sure if they were actually married. He thought his name was Ken, although he had no idea what her name was. It was a surprise to him to see her there, he had no idea they were in a similar situation to him. He made sure though to keep his head down. Pat was a proud man and he didn't want anyone to know he was getting welfare from his locality. It was bad enough having to face up to the indignity of having to queue week in, week out to collect his money, but having others see him who knew him would make him cringe. He had never been unemployed and at forty-six, hated the prospects of it now.

Pat had worked hard during the boom. Sheila had stayed at home raising the gang: Ciara, Maeve and Brian. In truth, he had missed a lot of family life. His two girls were now teenagers and Brian was eight. He felt he had been a passenger for years in the home. One day they were babies and the next they seemed to be nearly adults themselves. It sometimes felt like he had a seat at the family table, but didn't really make an impression there. He had been a ghostly presence in their lives. He was gone at 7a.m. in the morning before anyone was up and usually he didn't get home until 8 p.m. at night.

He was his own boss and ran a small plumbing contracting business. Things had gone very well enough during the boom years; most of his jobs were on housing estates, where he would submit a group price for all the residential units. There was no shortage of work for several years, but things started to dry up late in 2007 and early in 2008. Pat had three lads working for him; one, another plumber, and two apprentices. By July of 2008, he had to let the junior apprentice go and two months later the senior one. He had no choice; there was just no work for them. He had felt bad about this as they were trying to train for a career, but not as bad as he felt when he had to let Tim go, on the day they broke for Christmas holidays. Tim had just bought his first house and was engaged to be married. He was qualified five years as a plumber and he was a solid guy who looked out for Pat's business like it was his own. Pat had felt really guilty all over that Christmas holiday.

In time, though, he didn't even have enough work for himself. All housing starts were on hold. There was a glut of new houses on the market and they would need to be sold before any other houses commenced. Similar situations had occurred in a lot of other countries. The only work Pat could get now was the odd bit of maintenance on a boiler or small maintenance jobs on heating systems. He had been out of work officially for two months and decided it was time to register his case with the authorities. Their mortgage was relatively small, as they had traded up to buy their four bed in the plains and had released a lot of equity from their previous home. That was little enough comfort though when there was no guaranteed income coming through the door at the moment. While they had relatively good savings, they certainly didn't want to end up living off them for too long.

*** 

Jane had to make three trips to the welfare office before they even got her set up on the system. This incompetence infuriated her; if she had carried on in her job like that, she wouldn't have lasted a week. She smiled at the irony of it all. Here she was queuing for welfare, a highly efficient worker, and the inefficient older lady behind the counter was the one with the job.

I suppose it didn't help that she worked in a luxury business like public relations. In times of recession, all companies pulled in their horns and cut all discretionary spending. Despite the fact that she was extremely well connected in the city and was a genius at promoting products and businesses, it just didn't matter.

Ken and she had worked very hard for everything they had. Both Dubliners, they had chosen to move out of the city for a quieter life. They happened upon Hill Valley Plains on a sunny afternoon after they stopped at the local pub in the village for a drink. They liked the feel of the place and decided to make the move from their apartment in the city. Her work had kept her in Dublin late several evenings every week and on occasion, if she decided to have a few glasses of wine, she would stay with her parents who lived a few miles form the city centre.

Ken was a few years older than Jane. They had met in their early twenties, dated for a while and then drifted apart. She had spent several years travelling while he had lived in London working as an accountant. They had both being in serious relationships that hadn't worked out. They then both ended up living back in Dublin in the late 1990's. One night they bumped into each other in a Dublin pub and that was it, they were back together. Life was good for them and they had a great relationship. Children had not come up ever as part of their life plans. They enjoyed each other's company and had great friends. Marriage was never on their cards either, they were just happy as they were.

Luckily, Ken had his own business, offering accountancy services to small companies. While his client base had definitely shrunk, he was at least still making an income. He had the privilege of working from home if he chose, although he did have a small office leased in Glenmore, a small town eight miles away.

Jane was adamant that she would register for welfare. She felt she had paid enough taxes and social insurance to be allowed to claim some relief on that insurance policy now. She was not embarrassed to be seen in the queue. She knew she would get back on her feet some day relatively soon and this was just a stop gap.

***

Over the summer weeks of 2009, it became easier for both Pat and Jane to receive their payments. Jane did eventually iron out all her logistical issues and prove she was eligible for welfare, while Pat lost some of his embarrassment at having to queue. A sense of solidarity set in among the people as they waited for their remittances. All conversation revolved around careers lost, the hopelessness of trying to secure work, or the fear of retraining. Politics came to the fore within seconds of any conversation and invariably came back to how the people at the top in business always seemed to walk away with golden handshakes. None of them were likely to be seen in any welfare office. While they knew discussing these issues didn't change the facts or improve things, it at least let them vent their frustrations.

One week in September Pat was in front of Jane. He had realised she didn't know who he was as they had come face to face several times by now. The queue was long that day and he turned and spoke to her. This was the third and most important event that changed life in BallyNotter forever.

***

Pat introduced himself and explained that he recognised her from the estate. She admitted to having no idea really who any of her neighbours were as she often left early in the mornings and arrived home late at night. They chit chatted about life in the estate and their families for a minute, but didn't mention the reasons why they were both in this building. It was a busy day in the welfare office and there were several clerks processing payments together.

As it transpired, they ended up being processed at the same time and they shared the walk back to the car park. Loitering for a minute, Jane raised the subject of unemployment and its devastating effects on one's confidence. Pat nodded in relief that she had broached the subject and started complaining about the bills still coming through the door even though there was no income to match them. He was particularly aggrieved at the annual maintenance fees that had arrived the previous day from their management company for the upkeep of the infrastructure of the housing estate.

After completing construction of Hill Valley Plains, Kevin Maguire had handed the maintenance and upkeep of the estate over to a management company, A-upkeep Ltd. He had wanted to cut all ties with the development and move on to his next venture. There was a real legal grey area around the continued maintenance of housing developments, where often the responsibility was shared between the local council, the developer or a third party management company. Kevin's solicitor knew his reluctance to hold responsibility for this area and put in a clause that all purchasers of houses should pay an annual management fee. This fee was to be set by the management company, for a period of twelve years, after which it would go for review again. Of the forty-nine householders, only three raised it as a source of major concern on purchase, but they all acquiesced to the condition after a while. Everyone else just accepted it, thinking it was just a minor nuisance. It was judged that it was going to be around 300-400 Euro annually per household and this was deemed acceptable enough by the people back in 2003.

The only problem was that A-upkeep Ltd. was not very good at their job. They completed the bare minimum of maintenance, comprising infrequent common area grass cutting, minimal planting, and occasional replacement of street lighting bulbs (after much prompting from the householders). Their fees were rising every year and now stood at 720 Euro, plus VAT per household.

Jane's own blood boiled as she listened to Pat. Ken usually processed all bills and she hadn't realised how high this one had gone. It was then she connected the dots in her head and realised that these guys were providing a crap service for that. She had often peripherally noticed the unkempt nature of the common areas of the estate as she travelled in the car, but never voiced that opinion out loud to anyone.

Pat said he was just not paying this year. She tended to agree and made a mental note to make sure Ken didn't just pay it online as he did with most bills. Pat pointed out that these guys were getting nearly 40,000 Euro from them as a group annually, and judging by the return of effort, it seemed there was only a couple of thousand euros worth of value for this. The only work that seemed to be going on lately was in the last week or so, where he had seen that older man from number thirteen and the tall young English lad doing a good bit of clearing work over on the site boundaries. He wasn't sure why they were doing it, but now he was going to make a point of finding out.

They felt a sense of solidarity that they were going to withhold their fees after their conversation and they promised to speak about it again when they returned the following week.

*** 

3 Months Later
December 2009

Things had moved on dramatically since their first meeting in the welfare office. The bad news was neither had secured any employment, save for a few one off jobs here and there. The more constructive news was that both had been very busy following through on their commitment to abstain from, and subsequently evaluate their fees to A-upkeep Ltd. Pat had strolled over to Sean and Leo one morning as they cleared some brambles that had grown thick on the river bank. The two seemed to be quite content working away and Pat realised they had just taken it on themselves to do this work. Sean had never really felt the loss of the fees to A-upkeep and hadn't equated what they were doing as work that they were failing to do. His only goal was to occupy Leo and let the lad find his feet and learn to see that he could make a positive difference in the world around him.

Jane had been quite passionate in discussing the fees with Ken. Luckily for him, he had not paid them. She asked him to look into the history of them and he researched his bank accounts to see that they had been 390 Euro in 2003, and had seemed to rise by roughly fifty Euro a year until they now stood at 720 Euro for the calendar year 2010. I mean inflation was one thing, but this was hyper inflation territory. The issue had gotten his back up as well now. Ken did know one other man from the estate, Joe Kennedy, who was a solicitor living in one of the big houses at the front entrance. He spoke with Joe about the issue and again Joe admitted to not noticing the payment as it went out on direct debit from his accounts.

Joe researched the contract they had all signed and realised that it was flaky at best. While it did tie them into a twelve year contract, six of which had already passed, it also had promised excellent levels of care and service. They all agreed this was never met and so this company was in breach of contract. Joe reckoned they definitely had a case and that it was a sensible idea to pursue it.

Joe and Mary Kennedy had a very successful solicitors practice in the nearby town of Glenmore. Their business was booming. They had been handling a lot of receiverships and legal cases related to default of payments since the recession hit. Joe had felt awful about the human tragedies involved in these business failures and it pained him that his own business was profiting from peoples misfortune. He wanted to balance the scales a little and so offered his services pro bono on any case that may ensue against A-upkeep Ltd. This piece of news gave Pat and Jane the confidence to try and rally the troops of the estate together.

They spent nearly two weeks calling to the other forty-six houses besides their own. They thought they would only be a couple of nights at it, but once they knocked on the door of a house and introduced themselves, then invariably they found themselves invited in for a chat. Five minutes later the kettle would be on as they would outline their concerns over the fees. In all the houses people strongly agreed with them about the crazy levels of these fees once it was pointed out to them. Some were fuming that they had already paid, but vowed that they were not going to do so again the following year until the matter was looked into. After the two weeks were up and people had been encouraged not to pay the fees just yet, Pat and Jane set about planning to have a community meeting. It had been hard to find a suitable time to get all the residents from the estate to meet, but eventually, Tuesday night 1st December was decided on.

***

Pat rang Jane to confirm that she would take the lead in the meeting. He really was very nervous now that the day had arrived. He had never done something like this before, where he had to stand up to speak in front of a room full of people with all eyes trained on him. He had done it on his wedding day alright, but several pints of Guinness had taken away his nerves that day. Jane assured him all would be well. She did things like this every day in her old job. She often felt a tingle of nerves right before grabbing a microphone, but once she started to speak they all dissipated.

They met in the main hotel in Glenmore. It was a huge success. The delays in finding a suitable date for the group meeting had proven to be a major bonus as it had given them a chance to write to, and then meet with the management company regarding the issues they had to raise.

Pat had spent a week taking photographic evidence of the neglect around the estate prior to the meeting with A-upkeep. He had received a written affidavit from Sean stating that he and Leo had put in nearly 200 hours work in the past three months performing tasks that should have already been done.

Joe, Pat and Jane had sat one afternoon in late November with the slick executive from the management company. He still had all the airs of the boom; the brash confidence, the pin stripped suit and the styled hair to try and enforce both his youth and his own feelings of superiority. He waffled for half an hour about policy details, but it was all bluster. They were ready for him. He hadn't expected the professional and hard facts the team laid out on the table for him. He quickly backed down and agreed to release the residents of Hill Valley Plains from the future contract commitments. They hadn't expected that response from him. They had expected his company to agree to upgrading their level of service and insisting on payment of withheld fees immediately.

They told him they would revert to him with an answer after their group meeting which was on the following week. While they personally wanted nothing more to do with this guy and his company, they wanted everyone else to agree.

After Jane introduced the meeting, Pat spoke about their meeting with A-upkeep. His nervousness didn't hold him back once he realised he had a powerful message to convey.

They then asked for a group vote on pulling out en masse from the contract. All hands in the room rose. That was it, simple as that. Their association with A-upkeep was over. Joe Kennedy wrote to the director later that week to inform him of this fact.

*** 

Since the room was booked for two hours and their discussion up to the point of the vote only took thirty minutes, they decided to try and implement their own plan for the continued maintenance of the housing estate. A request was put to the floor to ask what tasks people thought needed most attention. They listed the first eight items on a flipchart.

- Regular cutting of common area grass
- Maintenance of site boundary
- Clearing of heavy brambles
- Painting of entrance gates
- Regular cleaning of internal roads
- Fresh planting, especially trees

- Creation of a safe boundary for small children to play with no danger from traffic
- Replacement of street lighting bulbs when they went

Volunteers were sought to perform some of the one off tasks, like painting the entrance gates. Three sets of two man teams agreed to do these tasks. As for the continued general maintenance, Sean proposed that he and Leo would continue working as they were.

However, he felt that since the householders were being asked for 720 Euro annually before, then perhaps it would much more palatable for them to pay an annual fee of 250 per household. He thought that it was not sustainable to expect ongoing maintenance of the park without some little pool of money backing it up. Amazingly, the group agreed by a majority vote to this. Pooling forty-nine houses generated 12,250 Euro.

Sean further proposed that he would continue working a couple of hours a day for free but that maybe Leo should get his nominal sum of 100 Euro from this kitty instead of from him. This wouldn't exhaust the kitty, but it would put it to work a little. They agreed, but felt they also needed some follow up meetings to track progress and to further plan what to do with the money. Sean had an ulterior motive in transferring his role as employer of Leo over to the community. He wanted the boy to feel some ownership and responsibility to people. It wasn't like the 100 Euro had been hurting his own pocket.

The meeting was winding up when a request came from Pat wondering who was interested in volunteering to form a committee that would be a fulcrum and driving force behind the plan. He volunteered himself, as did Jane, Joe, Sean, Leo, (Sean had raised his arm for him with a smile), Avril and a middle-aged lady who had sat quietly at the back of the room for the night, named Lisa. That made a total of seven people.

Fiona had fought back tears of pride at the end of the meeting. She couldn't believe the change in Leo over the past six months. Now all of these people were effectively hiring him without knowing him, based on the recommendation of an old guy they hardly knew either. This was a miracle for her, even though she knew he wouldn't be getting rich from his little venture.

***

June 2010

By the following summer a lot more was happening. The committee met regularly, about once every two weeks or so, and tended to meet in a different member's house each time. There had been about two more community meetings since the one in December, all in the hotel in Glenmore. The people of the estate were delighted with the progress. The place was looking fabulous. It had a real looked after feel to it and both Sean and Leo really grew into their roles. The painting was complete, the little play area was built—a timber enclosure with a lockable gate with some sand boxes—and all of these were completed voluntarily. The trees that were planted were paid for from the kitty but were planted with pleasure by several people one Saturday in March.

Avril had jumped on board with the whole project from the first night Pat and Jane knocked on her door. Her own life had improved immensely and both she and the kids were now far happier. James and Melissa now only spent two days a week in the crèche and as a result, she was also saving over half her previous annual child care costs. There really was no downside to her new arrangement. Her company was delighted, too, as her work was always early and finished to the usual excellent standard. She still pinched herself at how easy it was to re-jig the structure of her life to be able to let her operate from a position of power.

She had decided at a committee meeting in early February to tell the rest of the team how her own life circumstances had changed late the previous summer, when she had sat down to perform her detailed plan on how to break free from the 9-5 slog. She said she would like to look into a similar study for the families in the estate. The rest of the team fully endorsed her move, especially when she mentioned the several thousand euros she was now saving annually.

She set about her project with the same gusto as she had during her own plot to break free. She carried out a survey on all the householders that had pre school kids. There were eleven in total.

Here are her findings.

**The Smith Family:** Both adults work. They have two pre-schoolers, with crèche costs of 1200/month. Claire would be willing to work less time.

**The Logan Family:** Both adults work. They have one pre-schooler, with crèche costs of 800/month. Clara would be willing to work less time.

**The Finnegan Family:** Father works. They have two preschoolers, cared for in the home. Not willing for father to work less time.

**The Clark Family:** Both adults work. They have two preschoolers, with crèche costs of 950/month. Jessica would be willing to work less time.

**The Pradem Family:** Father works. They have two preschoolers, cared for in the home. Not willing for father to work less time.

**The Pratt Family:** Both adults working. They have one pre-schooler, with crèche costs of 750/month. John would be willing to work less time.

**The O'Leary Family:** Both adults working. They have two pre-schoolers, with crèche costs of 1100/month. Kerry would be willing to work less time.

**The Hogan Family:** Both adults working. They have two pre-schoolers, cared for by their grandparents. Cost 400/month. Maura would be willing to work less time.

**The Brown Family:** Neither adult working. They have three preschool children, cared for in the home.

**The Lee Family:** Both adults working. They have one pre-schooler, with crèche costs of 700/month. Mark would be willing to work less time.

**The Casey Family:** One adult working. She has two preschool children, with crèche costs of 1100/month. Sharon would be willing to work less time.

Survey as carried out by Avril on Preschool child care in community

There were twenty children in total under five years of age. Seven of those were cared for at home by one parent; their mothers in all cases. That left thirteen different children from eight households in crèches. This worked out at a total of 7,000 Euro per month or 84,000 Euro annually on childcare being spent by just eight households!

Avril sat with those eight households, seven of whom were couples and one divorced lady. Of these people, six of the women, including Sharon who was divorced, and two dads said they would love the opportunity to do something like what Avril had done, or even to just work a four day week to see their kids an extra day per week. However, moving to the type of arrangement Avril had created for herself just wasn't possible for most of them at their place of employment.

Avril had invited them to her house to discuss her survey. A flash bulb went off in her head again as she saw it all laid out before her. She excitedly told them that if they all managed to work one day less a week and co-ordinated amongst themselves, then they could possibly pool together and share the care of each other's kids.

Since there were eight of them, perhaps they could increase that pool to ten parents by including some other stay at home mothers. If they then split into two working groups of five, it would mean each working group would have to look after seven or eight children. If they all took one day a week off work, a different day of course, there would always be one parent from the pool available Monday – Friday to look after these seven or eight kids. Obviously, that would be a crazy ratio but perhaps each group of five parents could employ another helper. Two adults for seven or eight pre school children was a similar ratio to the crèches.

Now they could dramatically reduce the collective 84,000 Euro annual fees. They would need to hire two people of their own, but they could easily find some other individuals from the estate or outside to work for far less than that collective fee they were paying.

The upside was huge. The children would not be involved in rat races to crèches every day. The day would now have a much gentler pace to it, i.e. just walking to a neighbour's house every day. They would be spending quality time with their own parents, once every five working days, their parents would now be saving money and they would get to become good friends with their little neighbours.

Avril was beside herself with excitement. She only saw the upsides. However, she noticed some reluctant faces around the room. She probed further and realised there was an uneasiness in case it was a failure. They were worried that some of the other parents would not give the same level of care; they were concerned that two men were to be involved and most of all that it just couldn't be this easy. It always felt better to pay for a service like a crèche; at least then someone was responsible and accountable.

Avril had learned to listen better to people since she had gotten involved with the committee. She listened in earnest to the fears and after a while tried to assuage them. Here was her response and some questions she left the parents with to ponder on their own time.

- "Just because one pays for a service like a crèche does it guarantee your child is being cared for with the love you think they deserve. While their needs are being met, how special are they made feel"?

- "Your neighbour will make the odd mistake as will you, but since you are looking after each other's kids there is a mutual benefit to doing a good job"
- "It is imperative you do not become litigious at any point. Make sure to put whatever protocols you wish in place, but realise that this scheme can be for keeps, so if your kid cuts a knee playing do not ring your solicitor. It will kill the scheme for everyone"
- "Perform basic training in first aid and any other emergency reactions that are needed"
- "You are still hiring people who have experience working with kids so they will have experience of handling care for multiple kids"
- "As for the two brave men who showed up - ladies these are great dads who are brilliant with their own kids. We have to allow our men more into our world."

She had given them a plan. If any of the parents could manage to go part time, or if any were lucky enough to arrange a scenario like her own, then they could free up even more time to work for this co-operative of childcare. As it was, it could be successful with the minimum of reduction in working hours, just one day a week less. They could also add an hour on to their working day the other 4 working days to cover it if needed. After all, they were not rushing to crèches now.

***

Lisa particularly loved the model Avril had proposed. She had a huge affinity with children and was so delighted at the ultimate beneficiaries of a possible model like this, i.e. the little kids themselves. She had been widowed three years earlier and her own two daughters were living abroad, one in France and one in the UK. She had four grandchildren, two from each daughter, but unfortunately only saw them in rotation every eight weeks or so. Either her daughters came over to her for a long weekend, or she went over to them for a few days. She had considered moving abroad after Paul died, but how could she choose a country where one daughter lived over the other one. In the end, she decided to sell up their large family bungalow three miles from Hill Valley Plains and purchased a nice cute little three bed roomed house in the estate. Their old house had three acres and was a very mature site. It had been Paul's hobby, to constantly sculpt and evolve their land. In fact it was on one bright summer's day while he was pruning and clipping a hedge that the heart attack hit.

She did get a chance to say goodbye to him. She saw him fall from the kitchen window while she was making them some lunch. She ran and caught about two seconds of recognition from him before he left for good. Just as he did, she had the sense to tell him she loved him. She knew he was gone. Amazingly, there was about ten seconds of total acceptance on her part, where she just held him and rocked them both. Then the shock and grief hit her square in the guts and she ran for the phone to call an ambulance. They were there in about fifteen minutes, but he was long gone. She had tried to keep his chest massaged and give him mouth to mouth, but she knew in her heart it was in vain. The hardest part of it all was ringing the girls. How do you tell your child that their beloved dad was now gone? Paul and she had been together for thirty-seven years and although he was eight years older than her, they had been very happy.

Somehow, through all the raw grief she endured, she never felt cheated. She knew it had been his time and was so glad for the happy times they shared. The grief subsided in time and the move had actually been very good for her. The feel of the land in the Plains was lovely and it felt like a nice place to live. This would be the location for the latter chapters of her own life.

That December night when they all sat in the hotel function room in Glenmore, she had felt Paul's presence. She hadn't wanted to go along at all but that man and woman, Pat and Jane, had been very nice and persuasive when they called to her door. She did feel the maintenance fees were a bit steep, and eventually forced herself into the car to drive the eight miles for the meeting.

When Pat asked at the end of the meeting who wanted to volunteer to go on the committee, she couldn't understand why she raised her hand but yet she felt compelled to do so. This was the presence of Paul; after all, he had loved anything to do with gardening and she felt like she was honouring him by volunteering to help out, even though her bad back wouldn't allow her to do much in the way of pruning or digging.

Once Lisa had gotten the full run down from Avril on the scheme that she had dreamed up for the other parents, she vowed that she wanted to help them in some way. Lisa had trained as a child psychologist when she was younger. She never really progressed into a full time career in it, she had decided she wanted to be with her own two girls full time, but she still retained an incredible affinity to the healthy growth of small children. After all, ever since she and Avril had clicked at the committee meetings, she was calling over for a coffee every couple of days. She had fallen in love with her two little kids. She loved their company and felt welcomed into their home.

***

June 2011

One more year brought even more changes. Leo had enrolled since early February in a one year intensive organic farming and permaculture course in West Cork, much to the delight of his mother Fiona, who had willingly signed the tuition fee cheque. He had realised he couldn't keep working as he was; he needed to take a more solid step in life. It was a residential course and there were many varied and fascinating modules.

The principles of permaculture[1] are to organise and optimise the layout of the land that is available to you. It treats the land that extends from your own front door out to your site boundaries as a tapestry that can take myriad arrangements of food/tree/hedge/ shrub planting, animal rearing, domestic energy generation, water and waste recycling, optimisation of leisure space and intelligent design of services.

Leo revelled in his environment. He felt born to the lifestyle. It rained solidly for the first two months in West Cork, a common complaint in that part of the world, but yet he put on his dirty workman clothes and persevered at his tasks. The farm he trained on was nearly entirely self-sufficient, even though it was seven miles from the nearest shop. All food was grown on site. Animals were slaughtered for meat, eggs were collected every morning, and there was a never ending yield of rotating crops. They even managed to grow grapes, unheard of in Ireland, in a south west facing sheltered part of the land, where a greenhouse stood.

Leo realised that this was the perfect university for him. In time, he was able to see that this place was only successful because people like him came and studied here. If there were no students, then there wouldn't be enough people to eat the bounty and yield or enough hands to perform the work. In truth, the farm was not self sufficient until a collective of people made it so.

This was the light bulb moment for him. The only people living here permanently were the family that owned it. They had created a Garden of Eden and invited others to play and learn there. He lived somewhere that already had the collective of people, had the green land (21 acres) and now all it needed was a designer to inspire and forge a plan for their own Garden of Eden.

He kept Sean updated by phone on his progress and informed him of his plans to approach the committee with a proposal for a working permaculture model for the land in Hill Valley Plains. Sean spoke with Joe, Pat and Jane. They decided they would need to figure out some more about ownership rights for the common land. They contacted the solicitor of Kevin Maguire and requested a meeting. They informed him that they were a working committee of residents from the estate and that they had already negotiated to get out of their contract with A-upkeep. They now wanted to ascertain who had legal ownership of the remaining 21 acres in the estate. They knew they owned their own housing plots but were unsure of the remaining land.

Kevin's development company still legally owned the green spaces. However, it was useless to him as he could not build there anymore. It had taken several weeks of negotiations, but Kevin eventually agreed to a 99 year lease on the land at a modest annual rental rate. At the community meetings, it was proposed they all take collective ownership of the land. Again, reluctance set in amongst a few, but in time they all came around to the idea. It was decided that their annual subscriptions of 250 Euro could be used to meet the fee of 5,000 Euro for the annual lease. After all, since February they were no longer paying Leo his stipend from their pot of money.

They now started thinking about making some money from the land, and it was at this point that Sean was able to roll out the full extent of the knowledge Leo was learning on their behalf in West Cork. He was coming home for a holiday for two weeks at the end of August, and he had already performed some sketches for them on ideas he had for the land.

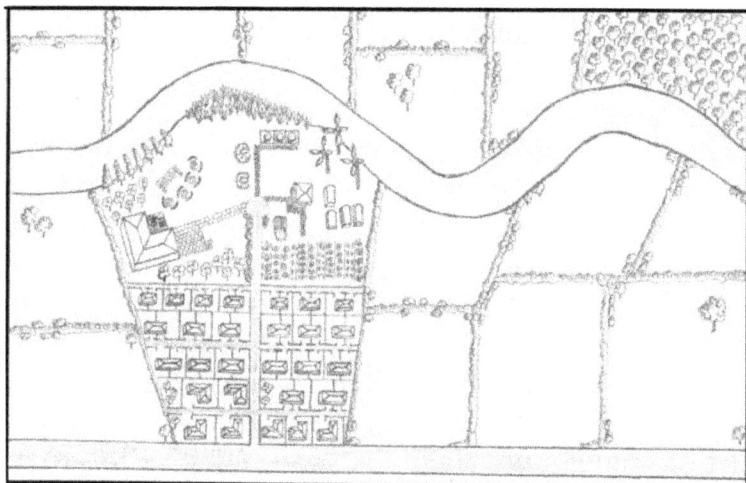

Plan showing some of the features of Leo's Permaculture plan comprising community building, shared food production, new planting and reed beds.
A full description of Leo's permaculture plan is outlined in Appendix B.

\*\*\*

One group of adults had decided to try out Avril's plan. Of the people she spoke with, six were sufficiently interested and committed to try and make it work. One of those was a man, Mark, who worked freelance in engineering. Four were working mothers and the sixth was an existing stay at home mother. Mark had the freedom to juggle his time and so was easily able to free up a day. Of the other four women, three were able to move to a four day working week at slightly less pay, and one moved to a part time working week of two days a week. None were able to arrange a working model like Avril's yet.

Their scheduling was a bit crazy at first. They made plenty of mistakes and the logistics took some ironing out. Initially, this group asked for help only from the estate and Lisa jumped at the chance to help out. She usually spent two hours with the children in the mornings. Sean had become a little lost again since the departure of Leo to Cork and so he asked if he could help out. He tended to go initially in the afternoon, but found himself going along earlier and earlier until his time there was overlapping with Lisa a little. He had really come to enjoy her company; she was such a warm feminine presence for all in the estate. However, they realised they would need a bit more full time care for the children and so decided to ask at the group meeting for any ideas.

Maeve, Pat's daughter and Alison, Leo's sister both ended up working for the group on a modest stipend. Maeve was in her transition year from school by now and Alison really was interested in childcare and had just finished her secondary school education. Both girls jumped at the opportunity to work so close to home, without having to get buses to Dublin every day.

In time, the other parents who had opted not to join the scheme saw how successful it had become. The parents involved were saving money and they also seemed far less stressed. The children, on the other hand, had far shorter days as they were not commuting and they were all getting cared for very well by the gang of Lisa, Sean, Alison and Maeve as well as by their own parents.

Community Childcare Plan

| Day | Parent in Charge | Staff | Helper |
|---|---|---|---|
| Monday | Sharon Casey | Alison 8*-1<br><br>Maeve 1-6** | Lisa 2 hours*** |
| Tuesday | Mark Lee | Maeve 8-1<br><br>Alison 1-6 | Lisa + Sean 2 hours each |
| Wednesday | Claire Smith | Alison 8-1<br><br>Maeve 1-6 | Lisa 2 hours |
| Thursday | Maura Hogan | Maeve 8-1<br><br>Alison 1-6 | Lisa + Sean 2 hours each |
| Friday | Kerry O'Leary | Alison 8-1<br><br>Maeve 1-6 | Sean 2 hours |
|  |  |  |  |
| Floating Parent to cover any day if needed | Deirdre Finnegan |  |  |

\* One of the girls showed up every morning at 8am but main parent was available before this time for any children that needed to be cared for earlier.

\** Cover lasted until 6pm but from 4:30pm onwards the children got picked up.

\*** Lisa was primary backup cover for either Maeve or Alison being unable to attend.

Nine Children being cared for in total;

Ciara 3,Mike 18 months, Laura 2, Dermot 4, Alan 13 months, Bethany 3, Sam 2,

Zoë 2, Abby 2.

***

June 2012
**Another year down with many milestones achieved.**

Joe had finished off all the legalities around formalising their estate into a co-operative. There were more efficient tax purposes for this and it also gave them a more steady footing. Jane had become choosier about her paid PR work. She wanted to make sure her clients had integrity and that they supported good causes. She also found a fantastic niche for herself in promoting the endeavours of Hill Valley Plains. Through word of mouth, several journalists had ended up calling by to do a story on various facets of the development, either from the design work Leo was implementing, he had graduated with flying colours, to the new childcare solutions driven forward by the parents. She handled all these interviews with aplomb. She then decided it was time to hold an open evening, which had happened in May, where they would showcase their ideas, their ability to find solutions for themselves, and their future plans to the wider community. People had showed up from all over the country; even some television stations from Dublin had arrived.

One knock on effect of the publicity they received was that many more housing estates in the commuter belt realised that they were clients of A-upkeep Ltd. They, too, were receiving equally shoddy services from this company. In time, the company was exposed as a sham. It had never set up any solid structures for maintenance and most of the money paid to it went on personal investments by the directors. The company went bust in a matter of months. However, considering how badly they treated their clients, it was ironic how that they ended up becoming a vital cog in the promotional machine for sustainable community. Because A-upkeep was so bad at what they did, it prompted many people to fix things for themselves.

Pat was back earning a decent wage, too, but he was also far more discerning about what he chose to take on. He had re-found his place at the family table with his enforced unemployment. Even though he greatly lamented the years of missed family time due to his endless time spent working, he vowed that he would be a strong and positive force in his family for the future. He had used his contact list to maintain his business once the recession finished and he then asked Tim, the plumber he had to let go Christmas week 2008, if he would be interested in taking it over full time. Pat would then work a few days a week for him. This suited them both as Tim had limped from job to job since Pat let him go and now he had the chance to run a trusted brand name in "Pat O'Brien Plumbing Contractors". Pat got the best of both worlds as he got to see his business continue, but had to commit far less time to it going forward. He would also get the free time for family life that he now demanded. Lastly, he was far too excited with the community projects in the estate to walk away from it all now and go back to long days of hard slog.

At a committee meeting in March, a few weeks after Leo returned from Cork, it was agreed that they should formalise a barter type economy. They would need to build a charter for the scheme. It would end up being a centralised listing of all the people who wanted to be involved in the community with a description of the relevant skills and services they were able to offer the group. Different people were obviously in different states of employment; be they full time, part time, freelance, retired, or unemployed. Everybody who was interested would be expected to only list skills and services that they had the time and desire to conduct for others.

Again this required some time to roll out. A single meeting in Glenmore was devoted to explaining the scheme to everyone. It was highlighted that no skill or task was too small. For example, if one was very handy at framing pictures then this was definitely something other people would need at some point. Obviously, there were very valuable larger skills, too, that would be fantastic if available on a bartering service, like plumbing (Pat), electrical (Mike), carpentry (Des & Adam), Fiona (nurse), Avril (logistics planning), Michael (IT), accountancy (Ken) and legal (Joe). These were just some people who had valuable skills that paid them a wage in the wider economy but that could be used to trade services in the local economy.

Personal integrity would need to be a cornerstone of the barter economy. But that being the case, there still needed to be a few ground rules. After much thrashing through they came up with the following.

- Everybody gets a chance to list all their skills – new people or skills can be added at any time or indeed removed if required. A database gets set up with all people and their skills
- Skills or services would be allocated points, maybe on a scale from 1-5. Depending on length of job and complexity it gets assigned one of the values above—a collective group decides point allocations
- Everybody sets up an account – ideally online
- This is a trading account, if one needs a service from the barter economy look online and see if anyone has that service or skill to offer
- Request work
- This is debited form your account once complete
- You are not obliged to return a service to that same person, however nobody is allowed go too deep into the red (perhaps 5 points is maximum). If it is the case that one has reached their limit then they cannot get any more trades until they either offer their services or a request is made for them
- People cannot ruin the scheme as the worst that can happen is their accounts lock up with a minor overdraft. It is not like one person can deplete the barter economy and then refuse to offer services back. Hence "bad debts" should be minimal.
- Nobody can build up too much credit either in their accounts. For example it is not practical to offer one service weekly to one person or household and build up high credits and then expect to get large quantities of work done by others in the community. A repeating transaction like

this should be part paid for with cash or should get far less weighting on the barter points system.

- These control measures were meant to ensure a continuous loop of work gets performed, i.e. nobody can deplete the system or drain others.

If everyone had to wait until they cleared their debt to just one other person, then the system would never work, hence the desire to make it a circular loop where your debt to one person is paid off by doing a service for another.

One other major benefit of a barter system is that it had the added benefit of meaning cash would become less and less important in people's lives as they didn't need to earn as much money to pay for goods and services. A lot of these services could be traded in a cashless, local economy.

Some people had gotten embarrassed at the meeting and shied away from the proposal. Sean had the sensitivity to see that it was most likely that these people had not had any formal education, nor did they have a formal trade. They felt like they had no viable skills. However, this was so far from the truth and on working individually one to one with them over the subsequent weeks he probed out lots of latent abilities.

The system was implemented and had teething issues, but in time became very popular. Some people decided to wait until it was at bit more secure before they joined, but in time, all houses had at least one person with an account. Not everything had to go through the barter system, e.g. people could offer a service for free or as a favour if they so wished. Below, one can see snapshots of the current accounts of Pat and Lisa.

| Barter Account of Pat O'Brien | | Member Number: 012 | | |
|---|---|---|---|---|
| Date | Transaction | Debit | Credit | Current Balance |
| 01/09/12 | 4 hours manual labour on grounds | | 1 | |

| 23/09/12 | Ken performed business annual accounts | 4 | | -3 |
|---|---|---|---|---|
| 01/11/12 | Fixing heating system house 23 | | 2 | -1 |
| 07/11/12 | Costing of material for community building | | 3 | 2 |
| 03/01/13 | GP visit to Bill | 2 | | 0 |
| 19/01/13 | 1 hour Public speaking tuition form Jane | 1 | | -1 |
| 12/02/13 | Fixing heating system house 12 | | 2 | 1 |
| | | | | |

| **Barter Account of Lisa Kiernan** | | **Member Number: 019** | | |
|---|---|---|---|---|
| Date | Transaction | Debit | Credit | Current Balance |
| 25/09/2012 | 8 hours weekly in childcare | | 1.5* | |
| 02/10/2012 | 8 hours weekly in childcare | | 1.5 | 3 |
| 09/10/2012 | 8 hours weekly in childcare | | 1.5 | 4.5 |
| 01/10/2012 | Internal rooms painted | 4 | | 0.5 |
| 04/10/2012 | 4 hours gardening completed on house | 1 | | -0.5 |
| 16/10/2012 | 8 hours weekly in childcare | | 1.5 | 1 |

* Even though it is 8 hours work a week it is only given to 8 families and could deplete barter system easily if it had a high

point count. Since Lisa didn't want cash for this service it had to get a low point ranking on barter system. She accepted this ranking. After all she could now get general manual maintenance completed on her house which she was unable to attend to herself.

***

June 2013

They had decided late the previous year to build a community building. It had seemed the logical move. Leo had made provisions in his plans for such a building. He was a key component of the barter system as his plans were just starting to yield food for the community. He was back taking a stipend from the community, and he also received small remittances in cash for the food he was producing. The rest of his work and pay was processed through the barter economy. Many people chose to put manual labouring assistance of his endeavours down as a function they could do for the community. So as he worked the land, he had a never ending cycle of different helpers.

They decided the building would be entirely community owned. Everyone was invited to purchase a share in the building, and also to barter services to the project to keep the construction costs down. The group only needed to purchase materials, and they did not have to hire any outside companies to help them with the build. Therefore, a 500m$^2$ building was built by the community for the same cost as a 200m$^2$ building contracted out to a developer. They took out a long term mortgage for the materials, spread over forty years, and it transpired that the annual cost for each household was less than 200 Euro. The commitment to pay this off would stay with the house, and if any houses were sold in the estate over the years, those incoming people would have to be okay with this. In truth, if anyone was to sell their house in the future, they would probably be making sure whoever was purchasing it was on board with the concept of a sustainable community.

This annual building fee, coupled with the 250 Euro they were still submitting to a kitty, meant they were still spending a few hundred Euro less per household than A-upkeep was trying to charge them four years earlier.

The building was constructed by early June 2013. It had several working rooms. The pre- school childcare groups stopped rotating among houses and took permanent residence in the building. The second group had now been formed, based on the success of the first, and the routines and schedules were firmly fixed in place for both groups. Obviously, some children were now at school going age, but they still spent a couple of hours after school in the groups. Of course in the interim, a few new children had been born to replenish the numbers lost to school. The monies saved on childcare, over 84,000 Euro by all parents, were used to employ two full time staff, Alison being one and another lady from the estate who had moved in two years previously. Lisa and Sean and a few others still gave a few hours to the groups, and it was part of the barter economy for them. The barter economy was really suiting Sean and Lisa, as they were getting older they could now get others to do more of the manual and physical tasks in their homes, while they returned the energy in other more socially oriented ways.

Romance had blossomed between these two during the year as well. They both had assumed an elder role in their society and were often approached by community members for advice. They found they had a huge mutual respect for each other and the paths that had brought them to Hill Valley Plains. They both felt that Paul, her husband, and Ann, his fiancée from all those years ago, had guided them to this location and to each other.

Sean, especially, did not think he could be so lucky. At least Lisa had had a happy life with Paul, but he, for whatever reason, had spent over forty years alone. He now realised, of course, that this need not have been the case, but he wasn't going to cry over spilt milk at this stage.

Fifteen small office spaces were allocated on the first floor of the building. These were set up as virtual work stations as more and more people in the estate were trying to work offsite like Avril. They had all taken inspiration from her path and several had made it a reality. However, working exclusively from a bedroom doubling as an office in one's home could be a little isolating.

Therefore, many people jumped at the chance to walk the very short distance to the community building to perform their career obligations, day or night time, depending on their preference. There always tended to be someone else around for company, too.

Provision for a common shop area and coffee shop was put in the building. In time, they hoped they may be in a position to sell some of the excess food surplus from the land in the shop. They felt a coffee shop would prove to be a great attraction, both locally and for the wider community. Lastly, they planned a shared communal space in the centre of the building. It was where they could hold their meetings, instead of trekking to Glenmore, and also where they could hold social gatherings in the future if required.

*** 

Of course none of this work happened in a vacuum without others noticing. All of the people living in Hill Valley Plains had friends and relations in the wider community and many had family and friends abroad. All of these outsiders ended up seeing the very real and amazing progress that was being made by the 150 or so people trying to make their lives more sustainable. In the space of four years, 2009-2013, they had set up committees, were maintaining their own land, were growing their own crops, had built a community building, were promoting remote working solutions, and had a comprehensive pre -school child care plan in place.

They had plans stretching out for around five years. A lot of those plans resolved around putting an alternative educational facility in place for children of school age in order to provide an alternative to mainstream education. They saw this as generating more local jobs, making their transport more sustainable, and most importantly, fostering and building their community spirit.

Of course, the bug was caught by others. As mentioned, A-upkeep Ltd, the stereotypical boom industry, had unknowingly provided a huge link into other communities in the commuter belt of Dublin. It was easy to explain to these communities about the benefits of decoupling from a company like A-upkeep and to prove to them that, from then on, they could dramatically improve their lives.

*\*\*\**

When Sean married Lisa in June 2014, he moved into her house. Since they were both comfortable financially, he decided not to sell his own home, but to offer it as a residential visitor quarters. Many people booked into his house, and into the spare rooms of other families, from all over the country, wishing to come and spend a week working and living in their community. They did this to learn from them and to bring this knowledge back to their own communities. Sean fed the proceeds from his leasing back into the community, as he could afford to, but others who leased out rooms used it as a supplementary income to allow them to further reduce their working commitments and hence their commutes.

*\*\*\**

Hill Valley Plains was not the only housing development to evolve a sustainable community from 2009 onwards. It acted as a catalyst for dozens of others around Ireland that mushroomed from the year 2013 on. In many other countries around the world, communities had started similar groups around the same time as Hill Valley Plains. The great recession of 2008-2010 had proved to be a major turn off for people to the existing economic model. They realised that the more they sat back and the more passive they became, then the more they would be exploited. In truth, if they stayed on the same path they were on, there would definitely be another recession within ten years that would probably dwarf that of 08-10.

The original gang of Sean, Leo, Pat, Jane, Joe, Avril and Lisa often had a chat about the unusual circumstances that threw them all together back in that fateful summer of 2009:

Sean spotting the vulnerable Leo; Avril saying enough was enough; Pat being brave enough to talk with Jane; Joe deciding to offer his professional services for free, and Lisa feeling Paul's presence to make her volunteer that night in December. Life was so intricate and complicated and there was an infinite amount of interactions with various people and places in one's lifetime. However, they would always remember the simple everyday events that changed their lives forever.

They were pleased, too, that so many other members of the community had stepped up to the mark. While our tale looked at the lives of the main protagonists, many other people were just as involved in the daily running of the community. Several other committees were up and running that dealt specifically with certain facets of daily life. All operated on a consensus model, where no decision that affected the life of the community was taken unless it had majority approval.

***

June 2015

Summary of their 2015 five Year Plan
- Set up recognised program for teenagers aged 14-18 to support their maturity into their future careers and adulthood
- Support community members who want to study in alternative education study, namely learning Steiner method[1] etc.
- When three or four adults have experience of alternative education policies then begin steps to implement it into the lives of children in the community
- Set annual targets on yields and crop type to be harvested from land
- Set annual plans in place for distribution of this yield and how much will be sold to wider economy
- Have at least one monthly social gathering in community building
- Keep working at perfecting local barter economy
- Track and target the ratio of mean household income earned from the wider economy to that of the local economy. As of

2015 this ratio was 90:10, i.e. 90% of mean household income in the estate was earned in the wider economy through employment with 10% earned locally through the local and barter economy. By 2020 this is targeted at 70:30, i.e. a trebling of the contribution of the local economy to mean household income. A direct relationship exists between this ratio and how successful the community is becoming at sustaining itself. This can be seen at the end of this plan from a study carried out within the community that had started at the beginning of 2012.

- Support community members to present information on development to wider community; namely PR, lectures, book writing etc.
- Investigate potential of purchasing a community bus, perhaps bio diesel, fuelled by non edible crops grown on river bank. This vehicle could act as communal transport for morning run to Dublin with an evening return trip
- Set target on renewable electricity production on site of 50% by 2020
- As the children of families become adults provision should be made for them to stay in the community if they wished, e.g. their parents could build flats on the back of their houses for their adult children or for themselves. Then when their children got married and had children of their own there would be space for all generations. This would keep families together, reduce the need for future green field housing and keep older generations safe and cared for by younger generations.

***

Study Carried out beginning in early 2012 (and revisited every year thereafter) into the success of the community in achieving sustainability, based on key Indicators.

| | 2011 | 2012 | 2013 | 2014 | 2015 |
|---|---|---|---|---|---|
| Per Capita Income (Eu)[a] | 22,538 | 22,040 | 22,184 | 22,134 | 21,540 |
| Local Economy Income (Eu)[b] | 478 | 832 | 1359 | 1,752 | 2,490 |
| Total Income per capita[c] | 23,016 | 22,872 | 23,543 | 23,886 | 24,030 |
| Sustainability Ratio[d] | 98:2 | 96:4 | 94:6 | 93:7 | 90:10 |
| Per Capita Hours Worked In wider economy[e] (Adults) | 39.5 | 39 | 37.6 | 37.4 | 35.9 |
| Security Index[f]– Was 4.3 in 2009 | 6.1 | 6.3 | 6.6 | 6.9 | 7.5 |
| Happiness Index[g]– Was 5.2 in 2009 | 7.9 | 8.3 | 8.4 | 8.3 | 8.5 |

a) This is the average income earned per person in the community from the outside wider economy for that year.

b) This is a monetary value put on the income generated per capita in the local economy. Since it is hard to put a cash value on barter transactions as there is no transaction of money, it was decided to quantify the value as being the money saved if that service had to be purchased in the wider economy. Example: For 2011 the figure of 478 Euro per person was derived by lumping all of the following together: the savings from maintenance fees to A-upkeep Ltd, the cost of hiring Leo, the savings from eliminating external childcare incorporating the cost of hiring Maeve and

Alison, the lease costs on the land and finally the annual subscriptions to the local community. Overall this yielded a net saving per individual of 478 Euro.

c) Total income is possibly the least important line item for the residents of the community in their study. Sustainability does not care if income has to constantly rise but more so that that income from either a local or wider economy can always be availed of when the individual so wishes. We can see the total income does fluctuate but what is much more important is some of the following metrics, especially the one around the sustainability ratio.

d) The sustainability ratio is simply the ratio of income earned in the local economy to that earned in the wider economy. In the case of 2011 this is 478Euro against 22,538Euro or an approximate ratio of 98:2. By 2015 it had risen to 90:10.

e) This is an indicator of how workload in the outside economy drops off when one starts to take part in a local economy. As people bartered their time and services it meant they had less need to work so hard in the wider economy to earn money to pay for goods and services.

f) This is a measure of how secure the residents of the estate felt in their ability to meet their daily financial needs, to plan for the future and ultimately how secure they felt in their careers and workplaces. On a scale of 1-10, 10 being the most secure the average result was 6.1 for 2011. Note: When asked based on their memories of 2009 this figure would have been a paltry 4.3 back then.

g) The happiness index is slightly different from the security index (more concerned with finances) in that it deals specifically with peoples happiness levels in their day to day lives. Obviously the huge positive changes in the community had a dramatic impact on this figure. We can see that for 2011 this figure is a very healthy 7.9, compared with 5.2 back in 2009.

The charting of these metrics proved to be an excellent and tangible resource for the community to track their progress, and also to help showcase their project to the wider world. They had a focus, and goals, and were determined to keep on improving on their sustainability ratio.

***

June 2020

Croí Na tuaithe was thriving. They had their renaming ceremony back in 2017. Kevin Maguire had done them no favour by calling the place Hill Valley Plains. As they became more intimate with the land, they just couldn't reconcile themselves with the inconsistencies of the old name. It didn't feel right. They put a plan view A3 drawing of their development in the main hall and invited all community members to pick a new name; one with meaning for their place.

James, Avril and Michael's son, was a soulful little boy. Although he wasn't so little anymore; in fact, he had turned eleven a few months back. He loved playing with his friends, but he also loved his solitude and often went off rambling on his own. He had lots of secret little hideaways and juvenile camps built around the extremity of their estate. He especially liked to spend time next to the slow moving river and just watch it go by.

He had spent an hour or two on his own that summer morning. It had been sunny and just as a cloud threatened to spit a shower on him, he decided to run up to the community building. He would go in and read a book or see if anyone was around to play some games with. It was then he saw the poster showing a map of their landscape and asking any resident to pick a name for the location.

It must have been the fresh burst of energy he just received from the sun, or just the clarity a young person can bring to a situation, but he went into the office and asked for a marker and proceeded to go up to the map and draw as follows.

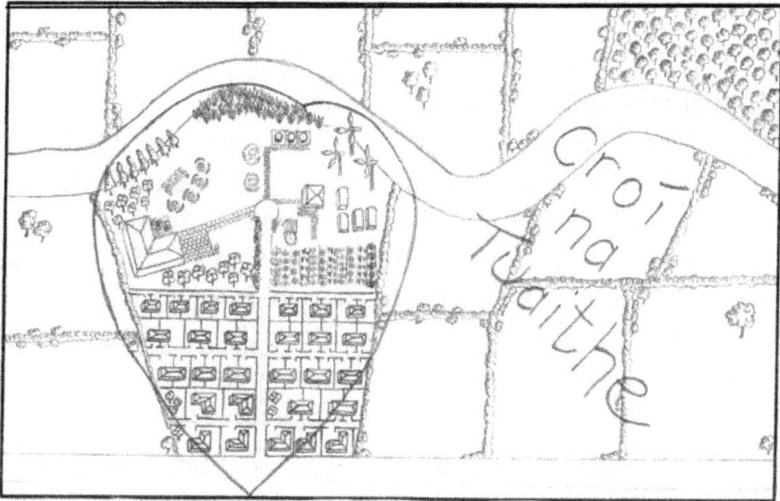

The "Vandalism" of James Cox aged 11.

Once he drew the heart enclosing them, he realised they would always be protected here in this place. His home place really had heart, and it also acted like a heart for the surrounding countryside, pumping out knowledge and support. So many people had come here to learn over the years and continued to do so. He loved his Irish lessons and was close to fluent in the native tongue. He then wrote the following across the sheet:

Croí Na Tuaithe. It meant heart of the countryside or heart of the locality and this place really did feel like this. Word spread quickly of the "vandalism". People gathered in the foyer of their shared building and many silently shed a tear in admiration and appreciation. They marvelled at the simplicity of what James had done and also for the sheer genius of it. None of them would have had that clarity or ability to literally get to the heart of the problem of naming this place like he had.

They didn't even announce a winner to the competition. Everyone instantly referred to their estate as Croí Na Tuaithe from that moment on. They then dealt with the relevant authorities, and even though they experienced the usual public sector blocks and red tape, they eventually persuaded them that their address had officially changed.

***

Leo was nervous that June morning in 2020. Even though Sean, his best man, kept him distracted and occupied with chit chat, he still couldn't believe the day was here. He looked into the full length mirror and saw the reflection of both of them in their suits and chuckled silently to himself. There he was, 28 years of age, 6'2", chiselled, tanned, fit and hardened from years of working outdoors. Next to him was his "best man", a 76 year old short, balding, but very cheerful man. If they were going to war, they would make an unlikely pair; a warrior and his Leprechaun.

Leo had thought long and hard about who he would ask to be his best man. He kept coming back to Sean, even though the idea seemed crazy to him. He did have plenty of friends, many from the estate, but many more from the course of his travels. He had become a recognised expert in sustainable community development; especially in the area of permaculture design and implementation. He had written two books on the subject and often travelled around the country giving lectures and practical demonstrations of his work. His life was busy, but fun. He still took great pride in guiding the work in Croí Na Tuaithe, but he didn't have as much time now as before to dedicate to it. He was more of a consultant to the development that an active member. That didn't stop him living there, though. He had long since decided that this place was going to be his home forever.

Sean had been the one to turn it all around for him and the man who always believed in him, no matter what. It could only be Sean, his best friend and best man. Sean was overwhelmed with joy when Leo asked him. His life with Lisa had made him feel like a young man again. He, too, had noticed the physical discrepancy in the mirror between him and Leo, but he didn't care as he was so proud of this young man and, anyway, he himself felt like a man of half his age.

Fiona, Leo's mother, had really gotten involved with community life over the years, but not everyone's life path meant they would stay in the same place forever. She had met a wonderful man a few years back and had decided she wanted to move to the city of Dublin to be with him. The community fully supported her and had a great party to see her off. Leo had bought her house from her and he and his sister still lived there now.

He had met his future wife, Claudine, all those years ago on the permaculture course in West Cork. She was French and, like him, was on the full residential program. They had been close during the year and had become lovers. But once that year was up, both figured they would never see each other again. They returned to their respective lives and started implementing their studies, he in Hill Valley Plains, as it was known then and she in a state botanical garden in Lyon.

About five years passed, they met again at a conference in London. The spark was there all that time and they couldn't keep away from each other over the three days. That was all that was needed. Claudine had lost the joy and the magic in her career that she had felt in West Cork. Everything was too regimented in her job. Leo sold her the idea of Croí Na Tuaithe over breakfast one morning, as well as trying to sell himself as part of the bargain. She moved over within two months and now worked side by side with him in many of his endeavours. In fact, she was more involved in the day to day routine of the estate than he was.

Their wedding was memorable. They held an outdoor celebration in the field alongside the community building attended by everyone from the locality and many others. Since it was mid-Summer, they enjoyed the warm sunshine all that day and evening until nearly 10 p.m. The party didn't need the sunshine, though, to thrive and it managed to last right through the night and well into the following morning.

***

As the decade of 2010's ended, the mainstream political and governmental organisations started to panic. Even though the recession of 08-10 was well and truly over, revenue from the people never seemed to rise significantly thereafter again. Populations were growing, but taxation seemed to have hit a plateau and was even starting to decline. This sent out a spiral of fear that was being disseminated from their PR officials. The message coming out was that we were all going to be doomed to failure as governments would not be able to meet their expenditure. This same message was coming from all governments worldwide.

However, what they had failed to realise was that the revolution had begun and they were still trying to cling to the old ways. Taxation and revenue had levelled off because the barter economy was thriving. People didn't need to work as hard outside the community to maintain their income levels as they were involved more and more in a transaction economy of goods and services locally. Therefore, there was less taxable income and, hence, less taxation going into the coffers of countries.

However, if one is becoming more and more self sufficient in one's own life, it follows that the community is also becoming more and more self sufficient and so *less* taxation revenue should be needed by government. People were now fixing a lot of the issues that government and public services had failed to fix for decades. So the old governmental models were now creaking at the seams. They had not adjusted their modus operandi. The people had risen up, taken on their personal power, and created better lives for themselves. However, government hadn't gotten off its ivory tower yet. They ended up trying every dirty trick in the book to try and re-instate the old system, tactics that were meant to scare the individual into breaking away from the power of the collective or the community. They failed in this and inevitably had to change to salvage some power for the future.

One classic example of where less taxation and revenue collection was needed was around healthcare. Before, countries poured billions and billions annually into healthcare spending. However, the more that sustainable communities integrated all the generations, then the less people needed medical intervention in their lives. Older people were starting to cost a fraction of what they had cost before to the state for medical care. A lot of elderly patients used to end up in state care as their families did not want to look after them. A cycle of despair set in and often one illness after another followed until they passed away.

Government didn't see this healthcare revolution coming and so still expected to need the same revenues as before. Unfortunately, many of these taxes were traditionally being wasted anyway in bureaucracy and mismanagement. This old system was crying out for more revenue, as before, to keep the dysfunctional cycle going, but the money was no longer available. The system crashed and had to reform to meet the needs of a different stakeholder. Healthcare of the future would need to be far more streamlined and deal more specifically with acute situations. This was because a lot of the medical care needed for the long slow declining health of patients of old was more redundant now. People led lives of new vibrancy within the community. The same situation would occur with reduced healthcare requirements for obese patients due to a revolution in food production and consumption within the future communities.

In time, the governments and brokers of power in our society had to realise that the world had changed. Just like all the great empires fell in history, the time had come again for another changing of the guard. The time of the "empire of the economy" dictating everything in our lives fell in the decade of the 2020's. A new future for the world was being birthed daily. It involved a life of individual empowerment and collective communion leading to a transformation of the human relationship with self and with mother Earth. The revolution started from the bottom up, in the process toppling the old system from the top down.

# PART THREE

# What if the Existing Path Continued?

Sean kept noticing that tall young boy as he walked to the shops in the morning. There was a time where he probably would have tried to break through to someone like him, but that was back in his own younger days when he had more energy. He just couldn't be bothered now with the hassle and the resentment he would most likely get from this young guy if he tried to help. He was sixty-five now, and had done his bit for society; after all, he had worked all his life with children. He wanted to just enjoy his retirement now.

Sean walked past Leo the morning Leo most needed someone to talk to. He continued on his march and an hour later returned to make his lunch. He sat that evening and read a book. At 9 p.m. his bed beckoned him.

The weeks and months passed by like this. He never spoke to anyone in the locality. The weekly visits from his family or to his family were becoming more sporadic. Eventually, they slipped out to monthly visits, and in truth, he didn't seem to mind too much. He felt he was a burden on people and didn't want to intrude on their lives.

The only life he saw was at mass on a Sunday or when he went and did his weekly shopping in Glenmore. Here he saw lots of people in the town flying by quickly, but it may as well have been a deserted town as far as he was concerned as nobody stopped to speak with him.

The years seemed to stack up and it was already nine years since he moved back up from Cork. It was 2012 and Sean was now sixty nine. He had found that winter tough; the short wet days followed by the long, cold and lonely nights. To an outsider, it would have been obvious that somewhere around October or November of 2012 Sean had resigned totally from his life. He saw no sense in moving on into another year of solitude and so the self destruct cell was activated on some level within his body.

On the morning of December 21, 2012, he left his body behind in his bed in BallyNotter. Ann had been there to meet him. The stroke had been painless; it just overwhelmed his body in an instant and the next thing he knew he was looking into Ann's beautiful face.

He felt all that love for her from the time they were together over forty years earlier. It didn't last long, though, as she showed him all the love he spurned and all the opportunities for happiness he had passed up. This hurt him greatly. He realised then that his life had been precious, did mean something, and in an instant he longed to return to the already decaying body in the bed in BallyNotter.

It was too late. Ann said she had been giving him signs for years to help him break out of his cocoon, the same cocoon he had erected to protect himself after she had died. The last and final sign she gave him was a few years back where she tickled his senses every time he saw that young English lad. She knew this lad needed help and had hoped Sean could break down his own barriers to bridge the gap. There could have been a wonderful ending to his life if he had taken this one definite step. He had failed the initiation. Ann still loved him and she didn't berate him in anyway. However, he had to face up to his life of missed opportunity and it was her duty to point this out to him.

It took four days for his family to find him. That is why he had waited until close to Christmas to depart, as he knew it could be weeks, otherwise, before anyone found him. They had to break down the door. They knew he was inside as his car was in the driveway and he was late for Christmas dinner in their house. It was a shock for them to find him like this and they all beat themselves up terribly for quite a while after. How could they let him become so isolated that he could die on his own like this and be on his own for four days?

\*\*\*

Leo continued to feel isolated. He failed his school examinations in 2009 and just to keep his mother off his back, went back to repeat them again the following year. He did at least manage to pass them and received enough credits to gain entry to a technical engineering course in Dublin. It wasn't a degree course, but at least

Fiona thought it would educate him enough to allow him attain a decent job.

He drifted through the next few years. He rarely went home to BallyNotter. To avoid awkward explanations over his absence, he got part time work at weekends and during the holidays. This meant he always had an excuse to keep himself in Dublin. After getting his qualifications, he ended up working as a technician in a factory in Dublin.

He socialised a lot with the gang from work. Over the years he had come more and more out of himself and he was the life and soul of parties in the pub. Alcohol became his lifeline, his crutch, and it allowed him to bypass the hollowness that he felt. Luckily, it never materialised into a full blown addiction for him. The sheer horror of the hangovers he suffered was probably what saved him from a path to alcoholism. He started dating a girl who worked in the factory with him and she ended up pregnant with his child. Max, his son, was born in 2016 when Leo was only twenty four. Leo vowed he would be a great dad and partner. He put his energy into it for awhile, but again, the emptiness caught up with him. Many years later when he was middle aged and living a lonely life in a flat, he often wondered why he started that affair when Max was four. His partner had found out a year later and kicked him out.

Of course the affair didn't last either. The upshot was that he lost all access to his son. His partner returned home to her family who were living in Galway, a city two hours from Dublin. Again, an outsider may have pointed out the intense irony in him absenting himself from his son's life at exactly the same age as he was (five) when his dad left him. His father had created a feeling of abandonment in him and he perpetrated that same feeling onto his son as it was the only thing he knew. He hadn't even fancied the women he started the affair with. In fact, she had meant nothing to him when compared to his own partner.

He never ended up breaking through his pain to understand the cycles at play in his life. He just kept a low profile, drifted into and out of relationships without making any commitments, and worked away in mind numbingly boring jobs in factories. This was his life.

*\*\*\**

Avril berated herself constantly. Life had become a never ending swing of emotions and a tug of war with herself. One day she beat herself up for letting her kids spend so much time in crèches and the next she beat herself up for the beating she had given herself the previous day. She couldn't win; she just couldn't come to peace with herself.

Of course the years passed quickly. Before long, James was well settled in school and then shortly after, Melissa started to attend the junior class in primary school. She was sure that once they were both in school that she would feel much better and far less guilty for not being there for them more. However, the feelings only got worse. Now they needed to be picked up by a child minder straight after school and brought to her house. They would do their little bits of homework under her guidance. They would finish this by the time either Avril or Michael collected them. This lady would also feed them and change them from their school uniforms into their own clothes. Avril had begun to feel like they needed her more than ever, now that they were in school.

Michael was able to collect them more and more as his career had hit a plateau and he was able to leave the office earlier than before. Unfortunately for Avril, she had created more complications for herself. She had gone for a promotion in work and had been successful. It meant another five hours work or so per week, all for the same money. She couldn't understand why she had gone for it; it just seemed like the thing to do, considering her length of service.

In time she just gave up. She couldn't see anyway out her predicament and so just gave up worrying and caring. After all, millions of women and men around the world were living her lifestyle. What was so bad about it? Her justification for giving up the battle for balance was that her kids would eventually leave home and she would be pretty lost then if she had no career.

By deciding to remain in work it meant that their weekends and summer holidays ended up being planned and filled up with all sorts of activities. She was determined to avail of every free second of time with her kids when she was not working. This was nearly more exhausting than the work week itself. She was always switched on, either working or working at family time. She was a stress ball and very unhappy. Every now and again she would slap herself, give herself a pep talk, and refocus again. This was her path and she knew she just had to endure it.

*** 

Pat vowed he would never be in this position again. Once he got back on his feet, he was going to work twice as hard. Being unemployed had ruined his confidence. Instead of availing of the new found free time with his young family, he had spent his days distracted, agitated and worried. His family was use to him not being around before he lost his job; but now he was a physical ghost like presence. He was there in body, but not in mind.

He ended up being out of work for over a year in total. Through all that time, he had noticed that woman from the estate in the welfare office, too, but he always kept his head low when he saw her. He sure as hell wasn't letting her know his circumstances. Anyway, it appeared she had no idea who he was.

He had become much more aware of his expenditure during his unemployment and was particularly annoyed at the bill from the management company for the upkeep of the housing estate. He delayed paying it as long as he could, but after the third reminder, he eventually wrote them their cheque.

When the contracts started to roll in again, he took to the road with a vengeance. He put in fourteen hour days and took on as much work as he could. In fact, he always took on more than he could handle and while he always had two or three irate customers screaming at him to start their jobs, he felt this was better than his competitors getting their hands on these clients. He was always playing catch up and the years just flew by. His two girls, Maeve and Ciara, ended up going to college, one abroad and one in

Dublin and then it was just his son Brian left at home with himself and Sheila. He couldn't believe where the years had gone, but now felt even more pressure to keep the money coming in since the girls had tuition and boarding fees.

When the world didn't learn from the great crash of 2008-2010, the next crash of 2020 was far worse. This time, Pat was fifty-seven. It chewed him up and spat him out. He was so busy trying to make money and taking on every job he could lay his hands on that he failed to realise he had over exposed himself to many developers who had gone bust. At least back in 2009 he was somewhat aware of the crazy boom that was going on and had made sure to get his contract payments before the tide went out. But this time around, it all happened so sharp and so fast he was wiped out.

Everything he had worked for in the past decade was gone. He found himself once more back in the welfare office in Glenmore, but this time it was going to be a much longer affair. He was never going to work again. His health had been broken and instead of long term unemployment benefits, he had to register for disability allowance. He was not fit enough to work. He was fifty-seven, but had the body and demeanour of a downtrodden seventy year old.

\*\*\*

Jane worked hard to get back on her feet after enduring eighteen months of unemployment that stretched up to the beginning of 2011. Ken had been a rock for her through the turmoil as she struggled daily with self worth issues. She had lots of free time on her hands during that period and since she didn't have any children, she ended up doing some voluntary work a few mornings a week in an old folk's home in Glenmore.

This work had made her feel part of something greater than herself and it put her problems in perspective. However, she soon found it very sad to see so many people in the latter stages of their lives struggling to gain any semblance of dignity and meaning. It was as if they had never lived a meaningful life. These people had been the ones to forge a path that all the younger generations followed. This was the way it has always been. Those who go before clear a path for the following generation, and then those people are expected to clear it some more for the next generation, and so on. It is why we keep evolving. It made no sense to her then to see all these people on the scrapheap waiting for death. It was a confirmation that they were not respected or appreciated by society.

In time, she saw that these people actually longed for death; after all, it was a release from their indignity and powerlessness. This scared her terribly. She was half way through her own life and all she had was Ken. While he was wonderful and she was very happy with him, she wondered what it would be like when she reached this stage of her life. What if Ken pre-deceased her? Would any of her PR associates, or even her friends, be around to support her at this time? Hardly, as even though they thought they were invincible now, they, too, would be old and weak at that point. Society just didn't have a place for old people. They were a nuisance.

This realisation really made her despair. She felt horrible and could only see a bleak future. When the contracts came up again at the beginning of 2011, she grabbed them and immersed herself in work for a while. She wouldn't look too far into the future ever again. Hopefully, society would change as she aged and things would improve for older people. Someone, somewhere, was bound to change things, right? She would get back to work and hope this was the case.

***

Lisa enjoyed her life in BallyNotter. She saw her family at the usual frequency and her grandchildren really were growing up fast. Her only worries in life now were for the lives of her daughters and grandchildren. She despaired sometimes at the way society was. After all the greed she saw in the years around the time Paul died, she thought people would learn and change their ways. But things seemed to be exactly as they were before. Now that it was 2013 and the recession was well and truly over, people were back running around like headless chickens. She was sixty-five and comfortable and secure enough in her own skin to take life at a nice easy pace.

She had got a shock in early January when the news broke that that poor old man from number thirteen had been found dead in his bed on Christmas Day, several days after passing. She had been away with her daughter in the UK for the Christmas holidays and only heard about it when she returned. It shook her greatly when she thought about her own situation. While she was only sixty-five, she realised that she, too, spent a lot of time on her own. This didn't bother her; she was very happy on her own, but she would have to think some more about this when she got older. She may, in time, feel the need to live with one of her daughters. She didn't want to end up like that poor man, or worse still, end up in a soulless nursing home somewhere.

\*\*\*

Hill Valley Plains did not age well over the years. It ended up becoming very shabby and unkempt. Maintenance of the common areas was always done to the minimum standards and grass was often overgrown and full of weeds. The children of the estate grew and flew the coup as soon as they could. There was nothing to stay for. After all, the place was just a bunch of houses one mile from a tiny village and forty miles from Dublin. What could they possibly stay for?

The irony was that they ended up moving from where they were to exactly the same type of place. They moved into shiny new housing estates in the environs of Dublin that were all as poorly planned as Hill Valley Plains. The same sense of dislocation and isolation was evident, and life was lived more and more within the confines of boxes; be they houses, cars, offices or shops.

And so the cycle continued. People had missed their chance to forge a new path. How many more chances would they need to be offered before they realised something needed to change?

# CONCLUSION

It's 2010 and mainstream society is tearing itself apart at the seams. Almost daily we seem to be living with unprecedented examples of corruption, lying, incompetence, negligence and apathy being displayed from the "elite" in our societies towards the general populace.

Any example of a mainstream institution, from our banks to our religious organisations, is proving to have had the interest of the individual and society at large as a minimal concern in its modus operandi. Even though this is the case, and we see the people on the street crying out for change, for accountability, and for more power, nothing much seems to be happening.

Why is that? Why are all our institutions failing us? And why is it that the more we demand accountability, the more we demand change, the more we spew our venom and anger towards those who so desperately wronged us and our communities, that the more things appear to be staying the same?

Wall Street is a classic example. Some would argue, with justification, that the businesses and banks located in this place (and in other financial districts) had a large part to play in our huge economic bubble and subsequent economic depressions world-wide. One would think that these organisations would be very slow to be seen to take large salaries, bonuses, post large profits, etc., considering the widespread catastrophic damage that their policies and operations caused. But 2009 was the year that some of these organisations posted their largest profits and paid out their largest bonuses ever to their staff. So in reality, these people make money on the way up and are smart enough and have sufficient political lobbying to also make vast amounts of money on the way down again. It is hugely ironic that many of these organisations offered "expertise" payable in huge fees from governments, with your money, to help unravel and quantify the extent of the mess that they had actually helped to cause in the first place. It is so farcical to be almost comedic.

It looks like we can't change things, right? These people and others like them, i.e. governments, religious institutions, etc., will always put one over on us, one way or another. We will never be able to change them.

Well, if we expect to change them the way we have been doing to date, then we will never succeed. We stand at the side and wail, moan and bitch about these people. We blame them for all our woes. We feel aggrieved and violated. How could they do this to us? Well my answer to that last question is how could they not do this to us? We gave them all our power. We still give them all our power. Daily, weekly, monthly, yearly. These guys know we may complain now because things are bad and demand their heads, but pretty soon they figure that things will revert to status quo and we will all go back to putting our heads in the sand. Either way, they know we won't do anything to actually change matters.

So the answer is we can't expect change until we affect change. It will be a long process, but it has to begin somewhere. We have to begin our self empowerment and community empowerment today.

Only when we stop paying huge excessive taxation will governments learn to streamline and actually become efficient, innovative and respectful of our remaining taxes. We stop paying excessive taxes by forming barter economies that allow trading of skills and services outside of the tax loop. Is it morally wrong to expect to pay less taxes and to also expect bartering to be tax exempt? It is not wrong, if we are performing the social services for ourselves at our local level without expecting central government to perform these services for us. So no, we should only pay taxation for goods and services that cannot be met by the local community. We should pay our taxes, but only once we have the guarantee they are being handled honestly, effectively and competently. Now we are taking the power away from inefficient government. They need to serve us or not serve at all. No amount of moaning and self pity will force them to do this today. That is why none of our politicians seem to be meeting our needs. We elected them into office from a personal position of weakness, with the implied brief that they were free to violate us in whatever way they wished. They will only change when we change. We change by governing ourselves and utilising tools like a barter economy to enable this process.

Similarly, only when we stop investing and believing in our "market" economy will we see the kind of change we are asking for from our financial "gurus". Again, we spoke earlier of the dysfunctional dependence we have on population growth. We have all been told that to succeed, one needs to invest in the future growth of the market economy. This could be in the form of stocks, bonds, property or any of the other complex forms of investment vehicles available to us. Savvy people invest, right? In theory, there is nothing wrong with investments, but when everyone does it excessively in the belief that the future will always yield a larger return; (because, heck, that is what happens!) then we have a problem.

No further proof is needed than the recent world-wide housing boom. Everyone and their granny was purchasing, investing, or looking to profit from property. Nobody chose to look at the demographics and incomes. At some point, we would run out of people to sell houses to. The market economy is an extension of this. At some point we have sold as many goods and services as the population can handle. So as long as we blindly follow our old principals and relationship to money, then we WILL get the same results from our banks and financial "heroes". They take our money and pass it repeatedly to each other, in the process taking a slice each time. They assume you will be relatively happy because as long as the population keeps growing, at a certain point in the future, there should be more money there for you than you invested. Very often this is the extent of their actual expertise!

So how do we make these guys less powerful? Well by now I guess you know it's not by assuming they will change or expecting legislation to make them more honest. Whole careers are made in this industry by learning to tiptoe around legislation. We effect change by investing more in our local community (e.g. building shared community buildings or investing in local permaculture solutions), not solely in the market economy. We usually invest in the market economy to assure us of security as we grow older. If we had more integration of elderly people into our society, more opportunities for them to "earn" money from the local community, and ensured they truly believed that they had security of resources throughout their lives, then they would feel less inclined to work so hard to invest in the markets. Now we see that these roulette players, finance professionals, have far less of our money to play with. Now they have to change, as the gravy train will have broken down. We have hurt them where it matters, in the pocket. Real change that is effective.

These are two classic examples of how we can change; a quiet revolution that will catch these guys unaware. No more whining from the sidelines that the big boys won't let us play ball. Let's just move to another field and start our own game. In time, we will have more players, more fun, and ultimately better lives.

Unfortunately, we can see that these changes will not be quick. It will be a slow process, but one that guarantees us a decoupling away from the incompetence, corruption and dishonesty that blights our institutional society.

\*\*\*

We spoke in an earlier chapter about how our governments and leaders do not make society plans. The one thing they tell us that trumps all other concerns is the economy. Our economy is our society, according to them. Unfortunately, even though they believe, (and run our daily lives with the well being of our economy as their guiding principle) they still fail to understand it, or even to come up with long term effective plans, goals and deliverables for that very same economy. They are clueless as to the actual workings of our economy. It has proven itself to be a multi-headed beast that has stubborn opinions of its own.

If we look at the world wide economic boom that predicated our lives for nearly a decade, from 2000-2008, we can see that the collective mood (especially in the western world) was one of exuberance, feel good and euphoria. All things were possible. This feeling drove the economy. Nothing could fail and tomorrow was always going to be a better day. Then as the light turned to darkness, low rumblings started about credit defaults, etc. The collective mood slowly turned to thoughts of uncertainty. In time, this collective mood has morphed into one of pure terror, hysteria, panic and downright depression.

It seems to me that our collective mood is the main driver of our economy. So why is it not possible to stop our fears, arrest our doubts and proceed to envision a positive collective outcome for our economy, and hence, for our sense of security in our daily lives? Perhaps the stark truth is that subconsciously we may not want to return to the old style of economy. Perhaps we know that even though we may have felt part of something that was great for a decade, that in actual fact, it was all a whim. We were not getting richer or more secure, but actually just getting more and more indebted.

I believe that this is why the current recession-depression is so confusing and continuing to linger. One month the USA may come out with positive economic data to indicate the recession is ending, while the European Union may come out with completely contradictory information. Then the following month the roles reverse, and the USA has a less than positive outlook. Similarly China, India, Brazil and other countries are all offering conflicting information. Basically, the economic experts do not know what is happening. They are lost. All reference points and previous indicators of growth are now up for debate. The reason we are seeing so much stop/start and false dawns on our way out of this recession is that the people are dipping a toe in the water one day, and then pulling in their horns the next.

As a society, we all want to return to a sense of security in our lives. However, deep in our hearts, we know that this old style economy will not give us this. No matter how many promptings come from our analysts, governments and from businesses to start consuming needlessly again, we are not so sure this time. Hence the analogy for the multi- headed beast above. One day we are driving forth out of recession, the next we plunge right back in again. I believe we are on a major threshold, and instead of choosing to return to the old ways, we are instead begging for an alternative path.

One thing is sure; we are going to have to make a decision one way or another pretty soon. We can't stay in limbo forever. The worry and uncertainty is too stressful and draining. Either we revert to type and resume consumption with a renewed vigour as our leaders would wish us to, or we start our new path.

We know the former path, while soothing our fears for a few years, is going to ultimately lead us to another huge recession in the medium term. The latter path is our great unknown, but offers us a tantalising taste of a life that could be so much better. Why dignify this recession anymore with wasteful worry, depression, and fear? Why not start our collective path to a more secure future by engaging with our local community and starting the process to regain our power, to determine our future?

It doesn't have to mean the end of society as we know it. We can still have our market economy that contributes a large percentage to our economic lives. We can still work in consumption related industries, purchase new gadgets, travel and enjoy the perks of modern living. We can do all of this, if we balance it with security in our lives, stemming from local economic and community success. How wonderful to never again feel like a job being lost or a company pulling out of a country is the horribly stressful life situation it is today. In today's world, losing our jobs makes us realise how little power we have, and ultimately, how little we have relied on our own resources or on our local community.

*\*\**

In the second half of this book we looked at the lives of some people in Hill Valley plains. Do you recognise them? I would think that the struggles of people like this are very common in the present age. Obviously, we haven't covered every potential problem that people may be facing in the modern world. However, we looked at a range of demographics from pre-schoolers right up to the elderly in the community and tried to make all of their lives better with simple changes. While some of the details of Hill Valley Plains and the problems people living there face may not be directly transferable to your own lives, in truth, they will tend to be pretty similar. As an example, you may not be experiencing problems with a management company in your locality, but with a local council instead. The detail is not important, what is important is that in either case, people realise they can take back some power themselves.

In time, the people of Hill Valley Plains (or Croi na Tuaithe) learned that they could be self governing and that they could feel greater and greater levels of security. This was inevitable as they realised that the community actually can, and does, meet many of their needs. They now feel less inclined to invest blindly in the markets and they also feel far less need to be governed. They are self governing and create part of their own wealth and security. Wealth for them will not be retiring some day from a lifetime of hard work with a pension pot of say one million euro, with nothing to spend it on except for rounds of golf with fellow retirees. Wealth for them will be their assurance of a meaningful place in society where they can still contribute into old age, but yet can also feel the security of being able to avail of goods and services from others. Of course they may still avail of a pension (and plenty of leisure time) to help meet their needs, but not one whose success or failure has only been linked to excessive market consumption.

***

Can the rest of us really forge a path like those people in BallyNotter? Of course we can. None of the changes the residents made in their lives, or those they planned to make in the future, were terribly complex. All of the people had the power within themselves to change their lives. Once they aligned their desire for freedom and self determination in their individual lives into the collective, then they became an unstoppable force.

It really is as simple as reaching out to another person to make that initial connection. We saw three sparks igniting the sustainable community development in Hill Valley Plains; namely Sean befriending Leo, Avril saying enough was enough and Pat and Jane communicating in the welfare office. Simple everyday moments that had the power to transform lives forever.

Opportunities like that, and others of similar ordinariness, present themselves daily in our lives. We just need to grasp the nettle and open our mouths to speak. Our words will then lead to action.

***

Another valuable tool in our armoury is that we can also learn from sustainable communities that have been operational for a long time in various locations world-wide. In most cases these were born out of a collective desire by the members to break out of mainstream society. There are some very successful long term communities like Findhorn in Scotland[1]. These people didn't agree with the way mainstream society was been run decades ago and felt they could do it better. Through trial and error and long term planning, they have set up co-operative businesses, built community buildings, have joint decision making, communal food production, on site electricity generation, water and waste processing and bartering systems. They are constantly evolving and adapting. Not only that, but the residents of Findhorn have trained thousands of people from "mainstream society" on many diverse topics over the years. This is often done on a residential basis to allow people experience true community co-operation and life.

Some of these communities may have initially started out as spiritual communities, but today, they have become very successful models for living in community with fellow man and the earth. While spirituality is often practiced strongly in their lives, they have also become very practical and excellent problem solvers in order to survive outside of mainstream society. This is evident by some of the solutions the have found over the years as outlined above.

So how do we get what they and others have? Well, we should look to a summary of their successes and failures to help act as a guide to us in achieving more sustainable ways as quickly as possible. What we should not do is assume these communities are more powerful or better than mainstream society in anyway. Therefore, we should learn from them but, not necessarily defer to them. After all, you, in your own life, are fully capable of deciding how to improve your situation and how to contribute more locally without replicating exactly what someone else is doing. Perhaps you have better ideas. Perhaps not. Either way, we need to share our resources (in this case information) more.

Conflict resolution would be one key area that communities like this have extensive expertise in, as once community is embraced, it will be inevitable that conflict will arise. This is probably the single most off putting thing for most people when it comes to community co-operation. They fear getting involved in conflict, or worse, being dominated by individual members. This ties nicely into the greatest personal thing we must do on our road to sustainability. We need to come into our own power where we won't allow ourselves to violate/dominate (or to have it done to us) others. Conflict is a guarantee, however, it is not life threatening. The healthy resolution of conflict can be, and is, very satisfying.

***

Millions of people worldwide live in soulless housing developments with hundreds, and indeed thousands of units. They quickly realise once they move in that their developments were never properly planned. By highlighting how a place like BallyNotter can become more self-sufficient and sustainable, hopefully I have given a blueprint on how any residential area can become more sustainable. For developments in a city centre, in a town, or even in a largely rural area like BallyNotter, we can see that the location is largely irrelevant. One could argue that in a city centre there may not be the green space like there was in BallyNotter to grow produce, but that doesn't look at the obvious solutions of retrofitting roof gardens on apartment blocks or reclaiming the green space of concreted courtyards.

A lot of people though in the green movement would turn there noises up at all the poorly built and ill planned housing developments of the world. To them, these are failed societies already, and so should be ignored. They prefer, instead, to look to the future and only concentrate on building new sustainable developments. We have to realise that we have already housed nearly all of the world's population. While we should make all of our future developments sustainable as a minimum requirement, it is far more important that we retrofit our society as we know it, i.e. we cannot ignore the chaos and poorly planned housing developments that have gone before.

The change to more sustainable communities and developments must happen in the near future. And, it will not happen in a vacuum. Once a few start to live like this, it will reach the masses very quickly. It will lead to less consumerism, less frantic working lifestyles, more co-operative efforts, and more social integration. People desire freedom and joy in their lives more than anything else. Once they taste this, they will never want to go back to the old system.

\*\*\*

The greatest thing we crave as a race is to feel needed, secure and that our life has meaning. Couple this with a feeling of freedom to choose our direction in life, and we have a perfect recipe for individual joy.

Once we find our own joy, then peace ensues. If we can achieve peace individually, it is inevitable we will also do so at a society level. We truly can come into harmony with ourselves and with the earth that hosts us. Those problems that seem insurmountable today, will yield resolutions with ease.

We have a big challenge ahead of us, but we are equal to the task.

## Appendix A

### Census of Hill Valley Plains 2010

| Number | House | Occupants | Occupation | Ages | Children |
|---|---|---|---|---|---|
| 1 | 5 Bed | John O'Shea | Electrician | 43 | Claire 10, Sean 8, Ciara 5. |
| | | Mary O'Shea | Homemaker | 43 | |
| 2 | 5 Bed | Joe Kennedy | Solicitor | 52 | Kevin 18. |
| | | Mary Kennedy | Solicitor | 51 | |
| 3 | 5 Bed | Maeve Murphy | Counsellor | 46 | Brian 16, Liam 11, Amy 9 |
| | | Billy Murphy | Policeman | 45 | |
| 4 | 5 Bed | Bill Johnson | Doctor | 53 | Joshua 19 |
| | | Debbie Johnson | Home maker | 51 | Ashley 15 |
| | | | | | Heather 13 |
| 5 | 5 Bed | Ben Hogan | Accountant | 39 | Dermot 4 |
| | | Maura Hogan | Acc. Manager | 37 | Alan 13 months |
| 6 | 5 Bed | Laura O'Regan | Nurse | 26 | All Single |
| | | Claire Hart | Teacher | 27 | |
| | | Lisa Hunt | Teacher | 25 | |
| | | Ann Delaney | Nurse | 26 | |

| 7 | 5 Bed | Michael Cox | S/W engineer | 35 | James 3, Melissa 15 months |
| | | Avril Cox | Logistics | 36 | |
| 8 | 4 Bed | Michael Dineen | Policeman | 44 | Kevin 12 |
| | | Nora Dineen | Home maker | 43 | Brian 10 |
| 9 | 4 Bed | Dan Breen | Retired | 66 | Adult children |
| | | Polly Breen | Retired | 62 | |
| 10 | 4 Bed | Paula Cronin | Administrator | 48 | Elizabeth 13 |
| 11 | 4 Bed | Pat O'Brien | Unemployed Plumber | 46 | Ciara 14, Maeve 12 |
| | | Sheila O'Brien | Home Maker | 44 | Brian 8 |
| 12 | 3 Bed | Geraldine O'Shea | Hotel Manager | 38 | None |
| 13 | 3 Bed | Sean Crosby | Retired teacher | 65 | None: Single |
| 14 | 3 Bed | Helen Ormsby | Widow | 58 | Adult Children |
| 15 | 3 Bed | Timmy Clark | Bank Clerk | 39 | Shauna 4 |
| | | Jessica Clark | Chef | 38 | Tina 2 |
| 16 | 3 Bed | Niall Murphy | Technician | 23 | All single |
| | | Tim Leech | Technician | 23 | |
| | | Killian Ahern | Technician | 24 | |
| 17 | 3 Bed | Evelyn Arnesen | Researcher | 35 | Amelie 8 |

| 18 | 3 Bed | Jonas Koch | Postgraduate students | 27 | None |
| | | Emilie Klein | | 25 | |
| 19 | 3 Bed | Patrick Bowe | Shop owners | 43 | Leah 11 |
| | | | | 42 | Donal 9 |
| | | Melanie Carroll | | | |
| 20 | 3 Bed | Peter Finnegan | Factory worker | 37 | Leah 3 |
| | | | | 37 | Owen 1 |
| | | Deirdre Finnegan | Home maker | | |
| 21 | 3 Bed | Mary Courtney | Retired (sisters) | 62 | None |
| | | | | 59 | |
| | | Bridie Courtney | | | |
| 22 | 4 Bed | Don Gleeson | Electrician | 47 | Molly 12 |
| | | | Home maker | 46 | Fergus 8 |
| | | Patricia Gleeson | | | |
| 23 | 4 Bed | Odhran Burke | Draughts-man | 42 | None |
| 24 | 4 Bed | Mark Lee | Engineer | 34 | Laura 2 |
| | | Lisa Lee | Surveyor | 35 | |
| 25 | 4 Bed | Patrick White | Factory Manager | 42 | Maeve 7 |
| | | | | 39 | Lorna 5 |
| | | Anne White | Factory worker | | |
| 26 | 4 Bed | Angela Lane | Teacher | 49 | None |
| 27 | 4 Bed | Sahas Pradem | Shop owner | 43 | Aalok 3 |
| | | | Home maker | 34 | Avi 2 |
| | | Leora | | | |

| | | Pradem | | | |
|---|---|---|---|---|---|
| 28 | 4 Bed | Kate Young | Engineer | 39 | Brendan 8 |
| | | | Home Maker | 40 | Daisy 7 |
| | | Brian Young | | | |
| 29 | 4 Bed | Pierre Van Den Berg | Importers | 42 | Pierre 12 |
| | | | | 41 | Antjie 10 |
| | | Joceline Van Den Berg | | | |
| 30 | 4 Bed | Con Leary | Retired | 63 | Adult Children |
| | | Mary Leary | | 61 | |
| 31 | 4 Bed | Darren Adams | Auctioneer | 40 | None |
| 32 | 3 Bed | Colm Brown | Unemploy-ed | 42 | Sean 4 |
| | | | | 39 | Luke 3 |
| | | Mary Brown | Home maker | | Penny 1 |
| 33 | 3 Bed | Connie Chalmers | French Teacher | 52 | None |
| 34 | 3 Bed | Fiona Smith | Nurse | 49 | Leo 17 |
| | | | | | Alison 14 |
| 35 | 3 Bed | Bob Kennedy | Engineer | 29 | None |
| | | | Sales | 28 | |
| | | Sheila Fagan | | | |
| 36 | 4 Bed | Ken Griffin | Accountant | 40 | None |
| | | Jane Brady | Unemploy-ed Public Relations | 37 | |
| 37 | 4 Bed | John Hennessy | Factory Worker | 32 | Single |

| 38 | 4 Bed | Mark Logan | Driver | 42 | Melanie 7 |
|----|-------|------------|--------|----|-----------|
|    |       | Clara Logan | Pharmacy assistant | 40 | Joe 2 |
| 39 | 4 Bed | Dan Hurley | Retired | 71 | Adult children |
|    |       | AnnMarie Hurley |  | 68 |  |
| 40 | 5 Bed | Adam O'Leary | Carpenter | 45 | Debbie 7 |
|    |       | Kerry O'Leary | Nurse | 40 | Zoë & Abby 2 |
| 41 | 5 Bed | Ted Curtis | Unemploy-ed Architect | 49 | Paul & Kate 7 |
|    |       | Barbara Dennis | Home maker | 41 |  |
| 42 | 5 Bed | Sharon Casey | Dentist | 41 | Ciara 3 |
|    |       |  |  |  | Mike 18 months |
| 43 | 5 Bed | Paul Price | IT consultant | 47 | Megan 14 |
|    |       | Kate Price | Unemploy-ed IT consultant | 45 | Johnny 12 |
| 44 | 3 Bed | Maura O'Shea | Hairdresser | 39 | None. |
| 45 | 3 Bed | Ken Maher | Garden Designer | 43 | None. |
|    |       | Liam Brody | Salesman | 37 |  |
| 46 | 3 Bed | Conor Duggan | Teacher | 49 | Emily 15 |
| 47 | 3 Bed | Pat Doyle | Postal | 55 | Jessica 19 |

|    |       | Una French      | worker                                   | 55 | Hugh 13                                    |
|----|-------|-----------------|------------------------------------------|----|--------------------------------------------|
|    |       |                 | Factory worker                           |    |                                            |
| 48 | 3 Bed | Lisa Kiernan    | Trained as child psychol-ogist           | 61 | Two adults daughters living abroad         |
| 49 | 3 Bed | Sean Smith      | Mechanic                                 | 38 | Bethany 3                                  |
|    |       | Claire Smith    | Receptionist                             | 39 | Sam 2                                      |

Appendix B

**Ideas from Leo about intelligent design and Permaculture principles they could adopt:**

• Each household to begin recycling organic waste in a centralised purpose built (low tech – hence very inexpensive) composting facility

• Dedicate a small percentage of each individual householder's site to food production. Average site size is 0.35 acres. Allocating 0.1 acre to food production would allow a variety and abundance of vegetable, herb and food production. When coupled with varying produce from other householders this would lead to a large bounty. Not all households have to manage this themselves. It could be farmed out to select members of the community who work exclusively in local economy at food production.

• Dedicate 6 acres of the 21 acre green space to food production. Apply the principles from individual householder plots to larger community plot. In total this allowed for just over 10 acres of organic food production. Fertilizer would be the recycled organic waste from centralised unit.

• Each household to siphon off their rainwater from their roofs. This could be stored in large tanks recycled from wider economy industries and act as water for toilets and washing machines or indeed water for the land during dry weather periods.

• Provision made for a shared community building with shared offices, shop units and shared recreational space. This will also incorporate indoor and outdoor play and cooking areas for community celebrations.

• A policy of crop rotation implemented whereby intensive study is undertaken to make sure the correct crops are planted every year to replenish the mineral levels of the soil.

This is because repeated cultivation of one crop type depletes soil health

- On site electricity generation. Investigation of cheap alternatives to commercially available wind and solar generating technologies. Cheap and effective wind turbines can be designed and safely built at a fraction of the cost of many in the market place. Plans drawn up for ten small to medium sized turbines dotted throughout the estate, contributing 20% initially of collective electricity consumption of all the householders. This could increase in time.
- Planting of lots of trees and shrubs along the river bank to act as shelter form the wind but to also act as soakage for very intermittent flooding risk from the river
- Planting of quick growing eucalyptus trees and fuchsia hedging along the entrance to the estate to act as a strong shelter belt from the exposed and windy south westerly direction
- Three acres set aside to grow biomass crops capable of producing bio diesel to power possible future vehicles.

# NOTES

Introduction:

1. 4% is the average GDP percentage increase per country (based on approximately 150 nations) from 1961-2005. Source: World Development Indicators database, Word bank.

2. In the UK from 1976 – 2003 this figure averaged out at top 1% owning an average of 21.5% of the country's wealth. Source: UK Revenue, http://www.statistics.gov.uk/cci/nugget.asp?id=2

3. Currently the world's population stands at approximately 6.7 billion people. All of the major population growth occurring in the world is from the developing countries. To increase our population the average birth rate per adult woman in the world needs to be 2.1 children. In many Western European countries the average is well below this figure. This means that in these countries the indigenous populations are actually falling and the only way for them to grow is to have immigration. For the next 50 years or so all the predicted population growth is also due to arise in the developing world, encompassing many countries in South America, Africa and Asia. However at a certain time it is predicted that the average birth rate in these countries will also drop below 2.1 births per adult woman. The timing of this is very hard to predict accurately but it is due to happen sometime after 2050 and before the end of the 21st century. The main reasons for the drop in birth rate would be due to increasing education standards and more and more proliferation of family planning due to contraception and knowledge. Many groups are working on accurately predicting when the actual date of maximum population will arrive and exactly how many people will be on the planet at that time but a common thread through all their work is that it will arrive post 2050 and before 2100 with no more than 10 billion people in the world at that time. The United Nations population fund is one of the main organisation (among many) carrying out this predictive forecasting.

4. "Each of us, in our own lives, will have to accept responsibility - for instilling an ethic of achievement in our children, for adapting to a more competitive economy, for

strengthening our communities, and sharing some measure of sacrifice. So let us begin. Let us begin this hard work together. Let us transform this nation", Presidential announcement 10th February 2007.

"For as much as government can do and must do, it is ultimately the faith and determination of the American people upon which this nation relies", Inaugural speech 20th January 2009

"And above all, I will ask you join in the work of remaking this nation…" Election night victory speech 4th November 2009

Part One:

Chapter 1:

1. People in community with others tend to work better together, are more intimate and are successful if they operate in groups of 150 people or less. This concept was worked through in some detail by Malcolm Gladwell in his bestselling book "The tipping Point". It has been shown that historically older native and indigenous communities of people worldwide formed themselves into groups of 150 people or less and worked with the resources of those individuals. This number of 150 is commonly referred to as Dunbar's number after anthropologist Robin Dunbar who conducted in-depth research on these community sizes. This is the key to sustainable communities of the future, i.e. the alignment of people into groups of 150 or so people for the same cause. However since our populations are so large we will see multiple groups of 150 people working side by side, especially in cities.

Chapter 3:

1. A United Nations GEO-4 report from 2007 proves that we are living beyond our means. The human population is now consuming more resources than are available. Humanity's environmental demand is claimed to be 21.9 hectares per person while the Earth's capacity is purported to be 15.7 ha/person.

UNEP's Global Environment Outlook: environment for development (GEO-4 2007) report.

2.  Not for any religious or spiritual purposes but I will refer to the Earth as she at times, purely for the concept of the earth being a nurturer and hence more aligned to traditional concepts of feminine energy.

Chapter 4:

1.  In the Western world especially people may have good jobs and consume a lot of goods and services. Unfortunately in a huge number of cases people are critically dependent on their next pay cheque. It is the only thing that can keep the show on the road. Therefore they end up trapped, whereby they do not have the financial freedom to leave a job and secondly they are highly vulnerable to getting sacked or made redundant from their position. They are often totally powerless. If they were to lose their jobs they often only have savings that could last them a matter of weeks. Even though they may be leading middle class lives of apparent security on the surface, very often it is a highly volatile balancing act that is going on behind the scenes. According to a report carried out by the Federal Reserve Board's Survey of Consumer Finances the average American family has $3,800 in savings with no other backup in most cases, http://www.washingtonpost.com/wp-dyn/content/article/2006/03/04/AR2006030400238.html.

Chapter 5:

1.  This concept in particular has been promoted strongly by Bernard Lietaer, an expert on currency and a strong promoter of sustainable economic models. He has proposed a new currency, called the Terra that aligns itself in value with a "basket" of commonly used goods. It is a model that takes the power away from currencies and their volatilities.

    "The future of money" (London: Random House, 2001).

Chapter 6:

1.  Report on working hours in various cultures, tribes and historical periods, http://www.eco-action.org/dt/affluent.html

2. Offices here are used as a generic term to describe many different places of work, e.g. factories, shops, banks, retail units etc.

Chapter 8:
1. It was the power of the few, namely the aristocracy, wealthy merchants and institutions of the time that kept both men and women in powerless positions.
2. One leading researcher in this field is Dr Warren Farrell whose work can be viewed at,
http://www.bestinterestofchildren.org/
3. Barack Obama's Father's Day speech 15th June 2008.

Chapter 10:
1. The NASDAQ, the stock market of choice for the high tech industries fell nearly 80% in the two years from 2000-2002.
2. An overview of European policy on the carbon credit scheme can be read at;
    http://www.ebrd.com/country/sector/energyef/carbon/index. htm
3. The EPBD, Energy performance of buildings Directive was implemented in Europe to quantify $CO_2$ emissions from buildings, while all car manufacturers in Europe are also required to quantify $CO_2$ emissions from engines.
4. The most obvious place to collect rainwater is from the roof of a dwelling, or any building. A basic formula where roof size multiplied by annual rainfall in that area minus water lost due to evaporation and filtration for cleaning will yield the total quantity available to a building. Example 100m$^2$ domestic roof in an area of 900mm of annual rainfall will yield 90,000 litres before any losses are accounted for.

Chapter 11:
1. The original message in all religions was usually outlined by a prophet who was said to inhabit both worlds, i.e. that of man and that of spirit (where they could converse with God and his

messengers), examples being Jesus, Mohammed, Buddha, Moses, etc.

Chapter 14:
1.  Complex carbohydrates are a necessary part of our diet. However most people fail to realize that these foodstuffs turn into sugar through digestion and sugar gets deposited as fat. So often we see people dieting eating low fat spreads etc. that are getting spread onto lots of doughy bread. It is not the spreads that are causing the weight gain, but too much of the complex carbohydrates. A balanced diet of meat, fish, vegetables, fruit, nuts and only some complex carbohydrates will guarantee an even weight loss that will ultimately lead to a standardizing of body weight.
2.  Thousands of medical articles talk about the relationship between depression and physical diseases. http://www.netdoctor.co.uk/diseases/depression/depressionand physicalillness_000601.htm
    http://www.valueoptions.com/spotlight_heart/html/pdfs/Arti cles/English/depression/depression_and_heart_disease.pdf
3.  Older people who feel they have contacts, friends, support and a role in society do live longer and are happier too. People of Okinawa Japan are a classic example of this. They often live to 100 years old in very good health. Ultimately it is down to living healthy independent lives surrounded by a strong sense of community. Life's joys and sorrows are shared with the community. http://www.4evayoung.com/okinawan-secrets-to-living-a-healthier-happier-and-longer-life/

Chapter 15:
1.  The earth has a magnetic system that is strongest at the poles but that radiates out over the entire planet. It serves to protect us from space radiation and solar storms. It fluctuates over time depending on activity in the earth's core which sets up the magnetic field in the first instance.

2.  7.83 Hz is the well known frequency at which the earth's magnetic field resonates. This effect is known as Schumann resonance and was first predicted by the German physicist W. O. Schumann between 1952 and 1957 and detected in 1954.

3.  Geopathic stress roughly translated as illness from the earth coming from Geo (=earth) and pathos (=suffering). It is a quantifiable disorder resulting from increased frequency levels in the earth's magnetic field. Thousands of published articles support its presence.

4.  There are many techniques used to heal lines of geopathic stress. The most non invasive and invisible method is one involving earth acupuncture, where a person will be able to locate the lines of stress using dowsing techniques and then neutralize them before they pass through a building.

5.  Radon Gas leads to lung cancer.
    http://www.cancer.gov/cancerTopics/factsheet/Risk/radon
    http://ec.europa.eu/research/press/2004/pr2312en.cfm

6.  The average European throws away 520kg of household waste in one year.
    http://www.eea.europa.eu/themes/waste

Chapter 16:

1.  "In 2006, non-OECD energy-related emissions of carbon dioxide exceeded OECD emissions by 14 percent. In 2030, energy-related carbon dioxide emissions from the non-OECD countries are projected to exceed those from the OECD countries by 77 percent",
    http://www.eia.doe.gov/oiaf/ieo/emissions.html

2.  An overview of European policy on the carbon credit scheme can be read at
    http://www.ebrd.com/country/sector/energyef/carbon/index.htm

3.  Methane is roughly considered to be 20 times more harmful to our atmosphere than $CO_2$ emissions, i.e. it is 20 times more effective at trapping heat.
    http://epa.gov/methane/

4.  A report by the Sierra club highlights how the 10 most polluted cities in the world are all based for the most part in

developing countries while the 10 least polluted cities are all in developed countries,
http://www.sierraclubgreenhome.com/featured-article/the-cleanest-and-the-most-polluted-cities/
Chapter 17:
1. A history of the Oil industry,
http://www.sjgs.com/history.html

Part 2:
June 2011
1. Permaculture was a term coined by Bill Mollison and David Holmgren in the 1970's. It is either a mix of the words permanent agriculture or permanent culture depending on the viewpoint.

Mollison, Bill & David Holmgren *Permaculture One*. Transworld Publishers (Australia) (1978), ISBN 0-552-98060-9.

Mollison, Bill. *Permaculture: A Designer's Manual*. Tagari Press (Australia).

Mollison, Bill *Permaculture Two*. Tagari Press (Australia) (1979), ISBN 0-908228-00-7.

June 2015 Five year plan
1. Rudolf Steiner (1864-1925) was an Austrian visionary in the area of holistic education, i.e. in the area of truly empowering children to develop into their true nature and roles in life rather than allowing preconceived governmental, societal or economic expectations dictate that future.
"Our highest Endeavour must be to develop individuals who are able out of their own initiative to impart purpose and direction to their lives". Rudolf Steiner
"to receive the child in gratitude from the world they come from; to educate the child with love;
and to lead the child into the true freedom which belongs to man."
Steiner "rules" for his teachers.

Part 3:

Conclusion:

1. Findhorn information found on website, http://www.findhorn.org/index.php?tz=-60   .

# About the Author

Barry Fitzgerald is an electrical engineer by training, who also holds a masters degree in renewable energies and sustainable building design. Apart from having fifteen years technical experience across a range of industries, he has also used his skills and training to help many individuals lead more healthy and sustainable lifestyles.

He firmly believes that the world is on the brink of a major positive revolution, towards a more people centric approach to life. He believes that the proliferation of local empowered sustainable communities will be the catalyst to help the individual attain security and freedom in their lives, while seeing a simultaneous de-leveraging of power away from incompetent, not fit for purpose, institutional organizations. Barry lives in Cork, Ireland and is married with two children.

Barry can be contacted via his website, a site that is dedicated to helping promote sustainable communities: www.buildingcitiesofgold.com

**ALL THINGS THAT MATTER PRESS** ™


FOR MORE INFORMATION ON TITLES AVAILABLE FROM
ALL THINGS THAT MATTER PRESS, GO TO
http://allthingsthatmatterpress.com
or contact us at
allthingsthatmatterpress@gmail.com

www.ingramcontent.com/pod-product-compliance
Lightning Source LLC
Chambersburg PA
CBHW071429090426
42737CB00011B/1614